# THE AWAKENING
# OF THE INDIAN
# WOMEN

'Radical and visionary, Kamaladevi's *The Awakening of Indian Women* deserves a place on feminist reading lists and in the wider transnationalist feminist imagination, where it promises to provoke and inspire. Among other things, it is a potent reminder that feminism is not an invention or prerogative of the West.'

Amia Srinivasan, author of *The Right to Sex*.

'To those who now say, women's rights are human rights, Kamaladevi offers a similar formulation: "The women's problem is the human problem and not merely a sex problem." She argues that liberty or franchise alone will not solve the problems of the majority of poor women; the world needed a revolutionary restructuring of class relations. Starting with a searing critique of imperialism and a challenge to the notion that white men can save brown women, the book argues that British rule interrupted India's capitalist development and prolonged feudal exploitation. Imperialism, argues Kamaladevi, caused the country's social and economic backwardness. The book also includes brief essays by Margaret Cousins, Sakuntala Thampi, Maharani Indirabai Holkar of Indore, Shyam Kumari Nehru, and Jayashriben Raiji. It is a rare document from the global first feminist movement, giving us a glimpse of how Indian women related to the nationalist movement as well as the international socialist movement. Written at the eve of the second world war, the book positions Indian women and their movements in the complex interstices of capitalism and colonialism.'

Samita Sen, author of *Women and Labour in Late Colonial India*.

'*The Awakening of Indian Women* gathers a cast of anti-colonial Indian women who probed at the feminist dimensions of nationalist and Marxist politics. Ranging across birth control, women's labour, legal status, art and education, this 1939 snapshot of Indian women's late imperial experiences is a powerful demand for global recognition of the injuries of empire and Indian women's agency.'

Lucy Delap, author of *Feminisms: A Global History*.

'This book offers fascinating insight into the formation and circulation of anti-colonial feminisms in the first half of the 20th century. Bringing together diverse essays by writers and activists from the Indian women's movement, the book highlights the –sometimes occluded – role of Indian women in anti-imperialist struggles. Throughout, the book creates a powerful vision of women's political activism as a multivocal and, importantly, transnational form, paying close attention to the intersections of gender, class, religion and race while also aiming to build solidarity across national borders. From chapters calling for accessible birth control to discussions of women's artwork, the writers offer engaging arguments across a wide range of topics, many of which continue to resonate today.'

Maya Caspari, curator of *Forms, Voices, Networks: Feminism and the Media*.

'Originally published in 1939, *The Awakening of Indian Women* is a fierce assertion of anti-colonial womanhood against the entrenched assumptions of imperial rule. Penned to accompany the prominent activist Kamaladevi Chattopadhyaya on her tour of Europe and America, *The Awakening* upends the civilizing claims of the Raj and instead places Indian women at the vanguard of a global revolution in women's rights. This served both to publicise the Indian nationalist cause and, more specifically, to challenge the leadership of imperialist feminists in the international women's movement. *The Awakening* reflects Kamaladevi's distinct melding of Indian nationalist thought, socialism and women rights and vividly captures the extraordinary sense of possibility experienced by anti-colonial women during the 1930s. With an introduction by historian Dr Sumita Mukherjee, this new edition brilliantly illuminates this compelling historical moment and the role of Indian women within it. Equally, amid ongoing interest in the status of women, the re-publication of *The Awakening* is a timely intervention that speaks to questions of intersectionality and decolonization within global feminism.'

Rosalind Parr, author of *Citizens of Everywhere: Indian Women, Nationalism and Cosmopolitanism, 1920-1952.*

LURID EDITIONS

Bristol

First published by the Everymans Press, Madras 1939
First published by Lurid Editions 2023

Set in Baskerville
Typeset by Eva Megias
Printed and bound in Great Britain by
Short Run Press, Exeter

A CIP catalogue record for this book is available
from the British Library

ISBN: PB: 978-1-7397441-2-0; ebook: 978-1-7397441-3-7

# THE AWAKENING OF INDIAN WOMEN

KAMALADEVI
CHATTOPADHYAY
& OTHERS

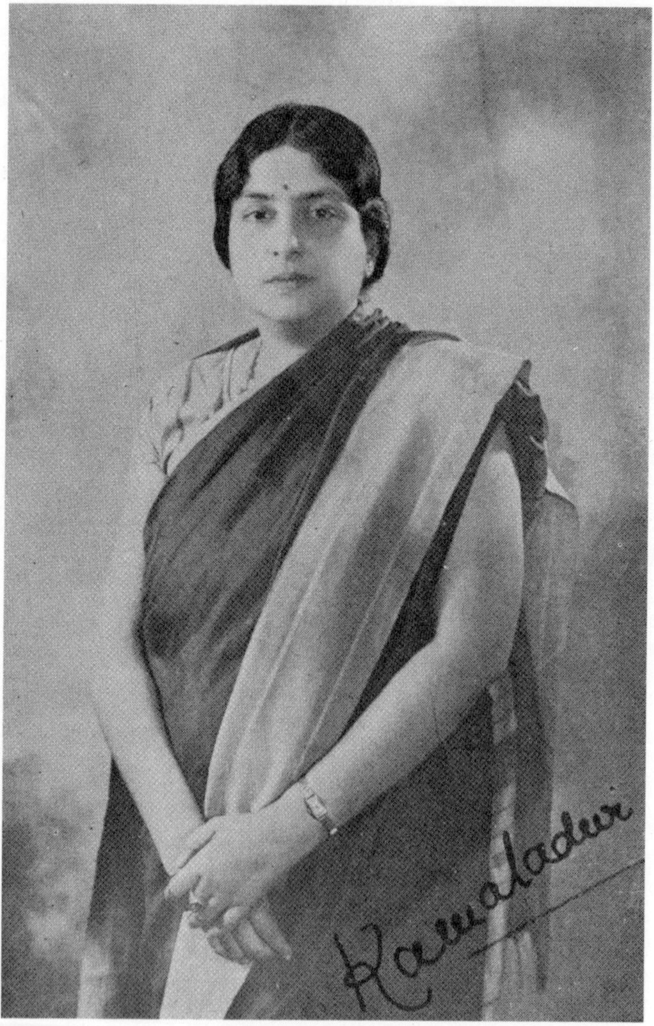
Kamaladevi

## Original publisher's note, 1939

THIS book has been specially compiled for men and women in the continent of Europe and the United States who may require information on the hopes, aims and ambitions of the women of India. In this compilation, Srimati Kamaladevi Chattopadhyayya very naturally takes-up a major part, for delineating the characteristics of the Women's Movement in India, while a representative group of eminent women write about the allied verities of women's sphere— of art and life and of the part that women played in the throes of the evolution of a nation.

# CONTENTS

# The Awakening of Indian Women
*Introduction by Sumita Mukherjee*

Kamaladevi Chattopadhyay was a leading member of the Indian women's movement during the height of the anticolonial struggle in the interwar period. She was one of the co-founders of the All-Indian Women's Conference, the leading women's rights group in India. She was also one of the early members of the Congress Socialist Party. When she wrote and edited *The Awakening of Indian Women* for Everyman's Press in Madras she was a highly regarded and prominent activist in the Indian nationalist movement and global feminist movement. Inspired heavily by socialist thought, her feminist-Marxist critiques bound through the pages of this book. As she puts it 'class-struggle is a historical fact' (pp. 49-50) and 'it is not liberty or franchise that will fundamentally change their position to their advantage but the change of the basis and entire framework of society' (p. 39). Known by her first name, Kamaladevi was keen to put together a book that would inform international readers about the vibrancy of radical activism in the Indian subcontinent and inspire support for the ongoing anticolonial struggle. Her key argument was that Indian women could only be truly emancipated with radical social change and the dismantling of colonialism.

Kamaladevi was born in 1903 in Mangalore, a port city on the west coast in South India. In many parts of South India, including Mangalore, there were some communities that followed matriarchal and matrilineal customs. This was not the case for Kamaladevi's family as her father, a district collector, died when she was seven and his property was inherited by Kamaladevi's half-brother, not Kamaladevi's mother. Despite her engagement with studies and the Swadeshi movement - a campaign that encouraged the boycott of foreign goods in order to prioritise Indian domestic and nationalist concerns - Kamaladevi was married young. Her husband died within a year. Kamaladevi is believed to be somewhere between the ages of 12 and 14 when she was widowed. Even though a piece of legislation known as the Hindu Widows' Remarriage Act had been passed in 1856, there was ongoing social opposition even in the early twentieth century to the remarriage of Hindu widows. Often widows were outcast from society. Despite this, towards the end of the First World War, she married again – to Harindranath Chattopadhyay.

Kamaladevi was introduced to Harindranath by his younger sister, Suhasini, whom she had met at Queen Mary's College in Madras, where she had been attending some lectures. The Chattopadhyays came from a well-connected Bengali family who lived in Hyderabad. Harindrath's older sister was Sarojini Naidu, a poet and prominent Indian feminist and nationalist who became the first Indian woman president of the Indian National Congress in 1925. She was a close ally of Mohandas K. Gandhi (also known as 'Mahatma' Gandhi), the leading figure in the Indian nationalist movement after 1915. Naidu was also leader of the Women's Indian Association and All-Indian Women's Conference and an important figure in the Indian women's movement and role model for Kamaladevi.

Soon after their marriage, Harindranath left Kamaladevi in India while he began a PhD in literature at the University of Cambridge. In around 1921, Kamaladevi joined him in England and enrolled on a social work diploma course at Bedford College (which had been founded as the first higher education college for women in the United Kingdom in 1849). She had initially considered joining the women's college Newnham College in Cambridge but due to her interests in sociology and social work enrolled at Bedford, and also attended classes at the London School of Economics. Meanwhile, the civil disobedience movement, led by Gandhi, was gathering momentum in India. Harindranath and Kamaladevi both decided to suspend their studies and return to their country. They returned via Paris, where they met Madame Cama, a prominent Indian women's rights and freedom fighter in exile, as well as 'Chatto' and his companion Agnes Smedley in Berlin. 'Chatto' was the name for Harindranth's older brother, Virendranath, a prominent Indian revolutionary exiled from India because of his engagement in seditious activities against the government.[1] As Harindranath put it in his memoirs: 'India seemed to call us back with an urgency which was inexplicable. We were glad we were returning.'[2]

1   Nirode K. Barooah, *Chatto: The Life and Times of an Indian Revolutionary in Europe* (New Delhi: Oxford University Press, 2004).

2   Harindranath Chattopadhyaya, *Life and Myself. Vol 1: Dawn Approaching Noon* (Bombay: Nalanda Publications, 1948), 221.

By 1923, Kamaladevi was fully engaged with the nationalist struggle as a member of the Indian National Congress and with the women's movement. She became friends with the Irish suffragist, theosophist and feminist Margaret Cousins and together they founded the All-India Women's Conference (AIWC), along with other leading Indian feminists such as Naidu, Sarala Ray, Muthulakshmi Reddy and Rajkumari Amrit Kaur. Cousins provides one of the short essays in *Awakening*. Cousins had moved to South India in 1915 and had initially co-founded the Women's Indian Association in 1917, leading the demands for Indian female enfranchisement. Cousins was arrested in 1932 for her support for the Indian nationalist movement. A stroke left Cousins paralysed in 1944 and she died in Adyar, Madras, in 1954.

Meanwhile, in the 1926 General Election in India, Kamaladevi contested for a seat in the Madras Legislative Assembly. Although Mary Poonen Lukhose had been the first woman appointed as a member of an Indian legislative body in 1925 in Travancore, Kamaladevi was the first women to contest any seats in the Indian Legislatures. A clause had been opened up for women to be nominated or elected to all Indian legislatures just before the election. In the end she lost by about 55 votes, although it is important to note that only 4.62% of the total votes in the 1926 General Election were cast by women. In 1929, she attended the International Women's Suffrage Alliance Conference in Berlin (with Naidu among others). This was a gathering of women from around the world to discuss the ongoing struggles of suffrage and political representation. Incensed that the Indian delegation would have to stand under a British flag, she and her fellow Indians cut up fabric from their saris to create a tricolour flag that was flown beside the others. In 1930, she was involved in the infamous Salt Satyagraha, when Gandhi and his followers boycotted a salt licensing tax. Gandhi launched the salt march in Gujarat and walked 240 miles down to the coast at Dandi in Surat, reaching there a month later to pick up salt from the sea. Kamaladevi was arrested for entering the Bombay Stock Exchange to sell packets of salt. *Awakening* was published in 1939 at the height of Kamaladevi's engagement with Indian feminism and nationalist circles and the height of Gandhi's civil disobedience movement.

Kamaladevi Chattopadhyay provides a compelling treatise on Indian feminism under colonialism alongside a withering critique of imperialism. *The Awakening of Indian Women* brings together a range of prominent women to offer a captivating history of the Indian women's movement prior to the partition of India and Pakistan. It offers a comprehensive overview of the Indian women's movement in the early twentieth century. Its attacks on imperialism and the patriarchy highlight the ways in which feminist thought was not unique or original to the west. Building upon her own education in sociology, social welfare and social research, Kamaladevi is clearly influenced by Marxist critiques of imperialism and offers her feminist-Marxist understanding of Indian society, arguing that India's economic and social development had been hindered by the British.

With any brief exposition of colonial rule and of the vast subcontinent, Kamaladevi often offers simplifications and generalisations. There are also at times utopian understandings of Indian society at large or in the pre-colonial period, with perhaps not enough emphasis on the issues of caste or sexuality, as was true of many of her nationalist counterparts. For example, Kamaladevi suggests that prostitution did not exist before capitalism, or that the system of purdah was not followed by Hindus, both of which do not accurately reflect the complexities of Indian society and the syncretisation of social practices within the region. She offers, as many nationalists of her generation did, a romanticised picture of the so-called 'Vedic' age of India, before successive waves of colonization, when women were purported to have had more freedoms than in the capitalist age. However, she is clear in her analysis of how western imperialism did not emancipate colonized women despite the rhetoric of the civilizing mission. Further, she emphasizes 'how successfully Imperialism propped up a dying society and gave a fresh lease of life to obsolete old traditions and customs under the guise of "Religious Neutrality" and sought to perpetuate their slavery' (p.11).

Kamaladevi presents vital discussions around the position of Indian women as they related to issues such as literacy, property laws, child marriage and the zenana. *Awakening* also offers useful contemporary insight into the major colonial and anticolonial activities in the subcontinent, especially of the 1920s and 1930s. Key to understanding much of the inequities of British imperialism lie in the laws and political structures they were responsible for implementing. These included the ways in which British colonial rule propped up existing property laws that disenfranchised women and the zamindari (landlord system) that perpetuated feudal land structures. The Government of India Act in

1919 introduced limited parliamentary representation for Indians for the first time under colonial rule but immediately and explicitly barred women from political representation. It was this Act which spurred Cousins and Kamaladevi in their engagement with the Indian women's suffrage fight and compelled Kamaladevi to stand at the first opportunity in the 1926 General Election.

The position and power of social reform movements is an area that Kamaladevi highlights in the book. For example, a key piece of reform that Kamaladevi discusses was the 1929 Child Marriage Restraint Act. This was the culmination of work led by Harbilas Sarda and the All-India Age of Consent Committee that set the minimum age for child marriage at fourteen for all girls and eighteen for all boys in British India. It was an act passed by the colonial government but very much as a result of the pressure put on them by Indian reformers. Kamaladevi campaigned to raise awareness about this legislation as there was very little the government did to ensure the Act was followed. This is just one example of the solidarity of Indian women with the nationalist movement, who often put the claims of anticolonialism first, as they recognized the need to rid themselves of the shackles of imperial patriarchies before tackling the insidious patriarchies within domestic India. The solidarity extended in including essays by other less well-known Indian women in Sakuntala Thampi, Maharani Indirabai Holkar of Indore, Shyam Kumari Nehru and Jayashriben Raiji to the collection. They cover important issues such as crafts, cottage industries, legal disabilities and the position of women in the household. The other contributors did not necessarily hold the same ideas about feminism or capitalism as Kamaladevi, but she was keen to produce a collection of essays that would counter the lack of information produced and published by Indian women at the time. Indeed, Kamaladevi's strident critiques did not reflect the wider Indian women's movement who were less concerned with issues of class or capitalism and more concerned with legislative change and representation.

The 1930s though were a decade of increasing civil disobedience led by the Indian National Congress, the main Indian nationalist party which Kamaladevi was sympathetic to; indeed, she played a leading role in its subsidiary group the Congress Socialist Party. As she notes in *Awakening*, key moments in that decade included the 1931 Karachi Congress, which epitomised some of the growing tensions in the Indian nationalist movement especially following the execution of Indian revolutionary Bhagat Singh.[3] At the 1931 Karachi Congress, Gandhi was put under pressure to respond to Singh's execution and show support for political violence despite his notoriety around non-violence. Within the Congress, Jawaharlal Nehru came increasingly to the fore of the nationalist movement as he introduced a Fundamental Rights and Economic Policy Resolution, which spoke to leftist demands for a combination of basic democratic rights, civil liberties, economic rights and benefits for all workers. Kamaladevi had attended the Karachi Congress and been involved in the discussions around the resolution. Soon after, Kamaladevi was arrested again in 1932 for picketing foreign cloth shops.

3   See Kama Maclean, *A Revolutionary History of Interwar India: Violence, Image and Text* (New York: Oxford University Press, 2015).

An ally of Jawaharlal Nehru and M. K. Gandhi, well-connected through her family and her in-laws, Kamaladevi was a highly travelled, engaged political activist. Though willing to critique Gandhi, the Congress party and the nationalist movement more largely – and especially attacking some of the conservative forces within Congress that limited its economic radicalism and limited women's participation - her critiques did not extend to the ways Gandhi encouraged a separation of duties for women and men, both within the home and within the nationalist movement. Nor did she deter Gandhi for how he discouraged women's economic independence. However, Kamaladevi's critiques of imperialism and patriarchal forces sustained her following the publication of *Awakening* and after the independence of India and Pakistan in 1947, when she became more involved in the arts and crafts and theatre movement, placing cultural production at the heart of India's economic revival. Kamaladevi's vision of placing arts and crafts and indigenous production as key to autonomous growth emerges in the chapters of *Awakening* and was to become central to her outlook after Indian independence.

Kamaladevi was All-India Women's Conference president from 1944-5. In 1953, she was a member of the Commission on Human Rights. After 1947, Kamaladevi became involved in the All-Indian Handicrafts Board and was an active promotor of handicrafts. She also launched the Indian National Theatre. She divorced her second husband, Harindranath Chattopadhyay, in 1933 – supposedly the first legal separation granted by the Indian courts. They had been largely separated from

1927 and they had one son, but he was mostly brought up by his grandmother. Kamaladevi died in 1988 and continues to be celebrated as a leading nationalist and feminist within India today.

*The Awakening of Indian Women* is an important example of the ways in which feminist publishing in the twentieth century was political and global. Speaking from India to international audiences, Kamaladevi had always been keen to ensure that people around the world were aware of the lively, engaged, and independent nature of the Indian women's movement, and to ensure that critiques of colonialism were being heard and understood around the world. It is a valuable historical text written by women actively engaged in the struggle for Indian women's rights at a time when the struggle for Indian independence was so vibrant and often felt so distant.

Kamaladevi was very keen to educate and counter the prejudices about Indian women that she had encountered in her own travels. In 1929, when she visited Berlin for the International Women's Suffrage Alliance and then the Prague conference of the Women's International League for Peace and Freedom, she was critical of how little the international gathering knew or cared about India and Indian women. She felt slighted and patronised. She was keen to highlight the injustices of British imperialism too and to forge new feminist solidarities. In 1939, for example, Kamaladevi visited Egypt and argued for closer cooperation between Indian and Egyptian feminists. Kamaladevi's publications were also a counter to the dominance of western ventriloquism and co-option of the Indian women's movement, as activist women especially in Britain tempered their feminism by notions of their superiority, whether by virtue of their race or imperial possessions. Indeed, many of the British contemporaries of Kamaladevi engaged in the international women's movement were keen proponents of the British Empire and failed to see how their calls for women's equality contradicted with their imperialist stances.[4]

Between 1939 to 1941, with the publication of *The Awakening of Indian Women*, along with her son Kamaladevi toured Europe, North America and Asia, which raised Kamaladevi's profile internationally. During her tour, Kamaladevi reached out to African Americans, including the National Association for the Advancement of Colored People (NAACP), keen to build up anti-racist and anti-imperial solidarities.[5] As the publishers put it, *Awakening* aimed to educate the 'men and women in the continent of Europe and the United States who require information on the aims and ambitions of the women of India'. Published in India though, it is unclear how widely read the book actually was. It was not widely reviewed beyond India despite the publishers' and Kamaladevi's intentions. The re-publication of *Awakening* by Lurid Editions in 2023 hopefully finally brings Kamaladevi's informed political thoughts and historical experiences to the attention of audiences she was always so keen to reach.

Sumita Mukherjee is a historian of South Asia and Britain. Her books include *Indian Suffragettes: Female Identities and Transnational Networks* (2018).

---

4   See Antoinette Burton, *Burdens of History: British Feminists, Indian Women, and Imperial Culture, 1865-1915* (Chapel Hill: University of Carolina Press, 1994).

5   See Nico Slate, *Colored Cosmopolitans: The Shared Struggle for Freedom in the United States and India* (Cambridge: Harvard University Press, 2012).

# ILLUSTRATIONS

# I
# Women's Movement in India

# II
# Imperialism & Class Struggle

By
Kamaladevi Chattophadyayya

# Women's Movement in India

## Man & Woman

At no time in the history of mankind have the suppressed elements and the long exploited forces been roused to revolt on such a vast and highly organised scale as the world has been witnessing since the debacle which followed the close of the war in 1918. In rebellion lies the seed of progress and revolts are as old as life itself, and the march of human evolution is marked by many an upheaval. But the revolt of today has a different character, because, life has changed its aspects so enormously since the Industrial Revolution shook the world. In the revolts of old, there was a lack of scientific insight and analysis. To-day everywhere science is adduced to justify ideology and action. The old-world standards based more on pretence than reality, on superstition rather than science and on credulity more than criticism, are rudely shaken. The man of yesterday is already tottering under the crushing load of make-believes and the man of to-day is fast extricating himself from the straight-jacket of hypocrisy or self-contradictions that irk human instincts—in short, he refuses to pretend to believe in God and yet serve mammon, hail himself a lover of liberty and persecute the champions of freedom, scorn sin with the virtuous airs of a saint and stain the earth with prostitution and disease. Man is learning to be proud of his humanness and does not seek to cover his honest visage with the superannuated mask of divinity.

In this general revolt, sex has played no small part though it is not usual to associate sex with social struggle. And yet, an intelligent study of civilization shows that the two are inextricably bound up. Sex attitudes are not independent of social and economic milieu but are shaped by the controls instituted by the classes that are dominant in society. The realisation of this is indispensable for a clear understanding of any social movement, particularly the women's movement, which, though apparently based on sex, has its real roots in the economic basis of society and woman's position is determined not by what is commonly called "civilization" or "culture" but by the entire framework of society.

For this purpose it is necessary to have the correct historical background for our picture, and a scientific perspective for tracing the journey of womanhood from the dim primitive age to the thrilling dawn of Soviet Russia, though the history of woman is not always a well ordered process on the traditional lines of evolution. While the status of woman does not reflect the prevailing intelligence of a society, it does indicate the nature of the economic life of the community and woman's position within it. Wherever we find woman economically dependent, we find her position inferior and subordinate, and wherever we find her economically independent, her position is elevated and advanced.

In the primitive society women very often enjoy advantages denied to their sisters of so called civilized society. They are more autonomous in their habits and attitudes because the economic structure of their society is simpler. Men and women share their labours and their gains. Hollow pretences do not intrude there with mock standards of false respectability to vitiate life. But with the rise of private property, kingdoms and empires, that simplicity is destroyed. More complicated economic forms take birth, the framework of society undergoes rapid transformation and the position of woman keeps changing along with it. Out of the insatiable possessive greed rises Imperialism with its passion for militarism and conquests and where warfare comes to be regarded as a male virtue, woman must necessarily get degraded, for, it is the enslavement of the forces of life by the forces of death.

The old simple life is broken up into a class-society with the leisured rich exploiting the toiling masses. Manual labour becomes a sign of degradation. The women become victims of this class-determined society, each rocked by its own disastrous forces. Thus, while the women of the richer classes lose their legitimate economic duties and their hands grow weak and helpless, as hosts of slaves and servants stand around to do their slightest bidding, their idle brains droop limp and inactive, and down amongst the toiling masses of women, the hands grow thin and coarse, the minds weary and exhausted. Feudalism comes with its aristocracy and its plebians. Thus, while the glittering walls close-in upon the upper-class women, gradually the basement cellar-doors clap upon the hungry working-class women: too little work and too much work both degrade womankind. It is class that determines the fate of women, not sex.

While men seek new pastures to enliven their idle hours and take to intellectual pursuits, they deny entrance therein to women. Woman is thus reduced to the status of a reproductive machine and while man's sphere keeps expanding, hers keeps contracting. Social function is no more recognised and she ceases to be an economic factor in society. When she ceases to be economically independent, she falls a prey to masculine dominance. She grows soft and dependent, needs protection and fences—in short, she becomes the private property of man and just as he seeks to fortify his other possessions by religious sanctions, ethical commands and legal codes, he applies the same measures to establish his dominance over woman.

Before Imperialism laid its dead hand upon our brave ancestors, women did enjoy a great measure of freedom and contributed not a little to the building-up of a fine culture. But a class-dominated society and the crushing heel of Imperialism slowly enslaved them—rich and the poor alike.

But it is to the upper class that we have to turn for studying social changes, conventions and codes of any society. For, in a class-society it is the ways of the dominating class that are accepted and adapted as the standard. Wealth subtly becomes a sign of respectability and the attainment of the style of that wealthy class, the ambition of the others. As in dress, so in social codes. This mentality no doubt has its exceptions and also receives rude shocks from time to time under the stress of desperate circumstances. But for general guidance

4

the rule holds good. New social codes and customs are introduced when feudalism rises and serve as fortifications behind which men entrench themselves to enjoy their undue privileges. Religions fall into line with this new social frame-work and create holy sanctions to maintain this order and to fasten the chains more firmly on women. Its chief characteristic is the absolute dominance of the whole stage by the Male with a capital M. Husband worship is a necessary feature of this. He is all-in-all to the women, all powerful, demanding unquestioned allegiance. Faithfulness to him becomes the supreme virtue and therefore marriage is the only and true vocation of woman and her aim in life to fit herself for it. The greater her submission to man and more the suffering at his hands, the surer and quicker is her road to heaven. From early childhood the imagination of man and woman alike is coloured by these codes and the women grow up easy victims of such philosophy. They are taught to consider themselves important only in relation to men and to fashion themselves on a pattern to serve and please the men alone with no individuality or mission of their own. Double standards of morality now come to be recognized: a severe code for women as the preserver of the social morals of society and an easier standard for the men whose fickleness and lapses are to be indulgently treated. Little does the man realise that in this are pregnant the seeds of his own decay. In a society which tries to render women helpless chattels of men, child-marriage and Purdah are inevitable, and along with it comes prostitution.

Wherever women have been economically dependent, morality has taken on a masculine cast. In ancient and

5

modern civilization the history of morality has been the history of male supremacy. Women have been ruthlessly ground under the wheels of masculine "morality," which in other words means a stern standard for the women and a light one for men. A multitude of devices have been employed to frighten and terrify the women and a variety of deceptions practiced to perpetuate their submission.

The more complex the civilization and sharper the division of classes, the greater the economic social struggle and the greater the trade in women. In primitive society the good of one woman was the good of all, the good of all was the good of one, for, it was a communal life. Prostitution was absolutely unknown. But the coming of private property and the growth of individualism tend to emphasise exclusive individual needs as opposed to individuality and personality: man jealously regards these as his own preserve and denies them to woman. Women who assert themselves and exercise their right to individual self-expression come to be regarded with disfavour as unwomanly. The ideal is henceforth the "Domestic Matron" which signifies not so much a high order of domestic qualities as rather a colourless submissive mind that has no opinions of its own.

Thus while the respectable virtuous "Females" are bred in the gilded cages, another class of women who sell their womanhood for bread is created.

The Industrial Revolution dealt a fatal blow to feudalism and in the upheaval which followed many new social factors raised their heads. Side by side, democratic revolutions such as the French Revolution, initiated a new ideology and a new philosophy of life. Those whom tradition and religion had long oppressed, saw a ray of hope in the new message and slowly the dumb grew articulate and soon the inert mass became convulsed into a mighty tidal wave that nearly shook the western world from end to end. Equality, human rights—new slogans filled the air. The long suppressed women found new champions to encourage and lead them. And there arose the Feminist Movement.

The history of women all the world over has followed these lines more or less though they may vary in many details. The history of Indian women is no exception. And it is against this background that we have to study the status of the women in India to-day and review their aspirations and ambitions.

# Enfranchisement of Women

The women's movement (in the accepted sense) in India as in the other countries is in the hands of the few bourgeois women who must necessarily maintain it within the framework of present-day society. It is consequently coloured by their own problems and needs and does not correctly reflect the demands or the problems of the large mass of women. This to a certain extent restricts its sphere as also lends a sense of unreality to some of its aspects. It cannot be denied, nevertheless, that there is a base for a women's movement though this base is wider than mere sex. It is largely conditioned and influenced by the present political and economic condition of the country, a fact which feminists are sometimes apt to ignore.

The working-class women, both rural and industrial are comparatively freer than the upper class women in India. Amongst the former, woman being an earning member and an economic factor, enjoys a greater degree of freedom. Economic stress compels this class to be less trammelled by severe social codes. Thus, while divorce and remarriage of widows is absolutely forbidden amongst the upper classes, it is prevalent in a customary form in the toiling masses. The same is true of child-marriage and Purdah. The problem of bread saves the poorer women from the dark dungeon of Zenana. As for polygamy, it is more a luxury of the rich than the custom of the poor. A poor man cannot easily burden himself with a string of wives. But the habit of borrowing the standards and codes of the wealthier classes still prevails and as a family grows prosperous this reflects itself in the gradual enchaining of the women folk. Thus, in South India where Purdah is practically unknown amongst the Hindus, it is very strictly observed by some of the Maharajas and Zamindars in their families. It indicates the status of the family, for the higher the class, the stricter the observance of the Purdah. It is this same habit which has spread the custom of child-marriage on so large a scale, irrespective of class or caste.

No class is really free from the social prejudice against women and the feeling that they are inferior. Therefore while the toiling masses are exploited as a class by the upper class, the women in their turn, even within that class, are oppressed and exploited by men. With all the economic freedom and legal rights which women enjoy to-day on the west-coast where the matriarchal system prevails, they are not much better than their sisters elsewhere, as they are still victims of social prejudices and superstitious traditions.

It is this which constitutes what is called the women's problems and has been largely responsible for the rise of the women's movement in India. But unfortunately the women's movement and its problems are not viewed from the historical, scientific perspective and the fundamental causes of these problems grasped. After all, social evils are merely evidences of the faulty basis of society, as diseases are the inevitable result of unhealthy living. We have seen that most of the social evils prevalent to-day in India are vestiges of the old feudalistic order which though in a declining condition, still exist in India. It is the semi-feudalistic form of society that is responsible for the crude superstitions and cruel traditions.

This is true of women of every religion in India. Just as the Hindu women who began as free and equal partners deteriorated into virtual slavery to men, so did the Muslim women also. They who had once roved the desert lands and shared the free adventurous lives of their partners sank to a chattel-status, completely at the mercy of men. Verse and chapter from holy books are profusely quoted to keep the women in chains, be they Hindus or Muslims. The just and fair laws of Islam mattered little. The iron hand of custom strangled them into inertia. Of what avail to them the kindly laws of inheritance and divorce to whom fresh air and sunshine were taboo? And though the Christian nations of the West may to-day talk with scorn of the down-trodden Eastern women, Christianity did not treat women any better: if anything it treated them worse. Rarely has religion branded women with such shame and humiliation as the early Christian Church did, laying at the door of a woman "The Fall of Man." St. Paul carried on a frenzied tirade against woman and sex as unclean things, echoes of which still linger in the forms of religious taboos and social prejudices against women.

The forces that shook the Western economic world naturally had their repercussions on the other parts of the globe. And we find a century ago, India too stirred by a new breath. Had India been left to herself, she might have worked out a great democratic revolution for herself after the decline of the Moghul Empire, and destroyed tottering feudalism. But the advent of British Imperialism deflected the entire course of Indian history. British Imperialism saw in this old crumbling feudalism a safe comrade. An alliance was immediately effected and its breaking frame rehabilitated. Little do those who think that the emancipation of the Indian women began with the coming of the British realise how successfully Imperialism propped up a dying society and gave a fresh lease of life to obsolete old traditions and customs under the guise of "Religious Neutrality" and sought to perpetuate their slavery.

The Indian Women's Movement as an organised current has differed in many aspects from sister-movements in other countries. For one thing, the progressive elements have had to meet with as much obstruction from the Government as from the conservative section. No national administration would have tolerated for a day the things which the Government of India chooses to ignore under the solemn cloak of religious neutrality. Nor is any attempt made to spread education and the light of science amongst the masses. Therefore, the fight of progress is an unequal fight. It is not merely against conservatism but also against the State which undoubtedly favours in its own interest, the continuance of reactionary forces.

The Indian Women's Movement has met with comparatively little organised opposition such as in the West where it was driven to take the form of a militant warfare. The Hindus and the Muslims have both a

11

happier background, for it was not so very long ago that their women were free to move about with them. But the early Christian Church with St. Paul as its genius created a very vicious tradition for the Christian Community and its evil vestiges linger far longer than any ordinary custom would. To this day the Catholic countries of Southern Europe are slower in giving equal status to women than the Eastern countries. And even in countries where women hold office in the State, the Church still resolutely shuts its heavy doors on women. It is the last citadel of man which he will not easily surrender, for then the religious awe by which women are suppressed and kept in check would be destroyed.

The Women's Movement in India has had therefore fairly smooth sailing. Although it began originally as a social and educational reform movement, it is fast becoming an all-embracing end. It was in 1917 when the Montague-Chelmsford Constitution was being drafted that for the first time the women made an organised effort to press forward their political demands. But the British Parliament, the bedrock of British conservatism, refused to concede their demands, leaving it to the Indian Legislatures. In 1918 the Indian National Congress placed the national seal of approval on the principle of granting franchise to women. The Indian Legislatures followed it up legally enfranchising and throwing open the Legislatures to women and rather startling the hide-bound British Legislators. Simultaneously some of the Indian States followed suit. In 1933 when a New Constitution was once again under consideration by the Joint Select Committee the premier women's organisation sent three of its representatives to place the women's case before it. The memorandum presented created quite a stir. It showed the enormous strides which political consciousness had made in the minds of the Indian women. They demanded a democratic constitution conferring full self-governing rights on India, including a clause in the Fundamental Rights granting equal rights to women, declared themselves strongly against communal electorates, against reservation of seats for women and special women's constituencies, against wifehood and literacy qualification for franchise. This reflects much credit on the sense of reality which the women showed in pressing these points forward. For the old franchise qualification was very restricted, being based on property, which under the present legal disabilities entitled few women to vote. The proportion of women voters to men varied between one to ten as in Madras and Bombay to 14 in Assam, a most discouraging state of affairs. But even the prospect of increasing the women voters would not tempt the women into agreeing to the wifehood qualification which was rightly resented as placing a premium on marriage and perpetuating the dependence of woman on man instead of recognising her independent right to suffrage. But all that the woman had condemned and objected to, found its way into the constitution; communal electorates, reservation on communal basis, special constituencies, wifehood qualification, etc. The literacy qualification is a mere mockery in a country where barely 2% of the women are literate. The total number of women enfranchised under the new Constitution is about 6 million—2,000,000 by property 4,000,000 by wifehood 300,000 by literacy. The proportion is 1 woman to 5 men.

Having successfully broken up the men into sectarian groups Imperialism has efficiently completed its task by cutting up the women also and not content with that has gone a step further and even segregated them from the general mass. Psychologically it is harmful, for it will create unnecessary differences in women and a lurking desire for special treatment. But that is all part of the imperialist game. Sex-bar has not been completely removed in the new Act. In fact, these disabilities are maintained as some of the blessings a civilized Government has bestowed upon them. Most of 700 Municipalities and 200 District Boards have extended the franchise and women members are to be found in them. This is a sphere in which women should be able to excel themselves, for, they deal with the primary needs of the public—needs with which women with their strong domestic instincts would feel more familiar and better equipped to tackle. But educational backwardness as well as economic handicaps prevent larger numbers from coming forward.

# Education and Child-Marriage

The political awakening among women received a tremendous impetus in 1930 when the Indian National Congress launched the Civil Disobedience Movement. Quick to respond to emotional appeals, the women were keenly sensitive to the call for service and sacrifice. Long oppressed, the word freedom worked like magic on them. Almost overnight they emerged out of their rocklike reserve into the glare of the battle-field, the turmoil, into the strange new world of publicity. The chains fell silently from their wrists and their tender feet which had never known the hard touch of open roads felt fresh strength. Hundreds faced danger, lathi blows and even gunfire. With pride they entered prisons, leaving behind the traditional sanctity of the homes which had sheltered them so long. It was a swift lightning process which had to be seen to be believed, to be understood. Ancient prejudices melted. Walls of tradition cracked and rays of new hope came creeping in. Even women who were still chained in their homes saw the rising gleams of a new life and a new world and their hearts leaped with pride and hope. A new dream of a better and a freer world slowly shaped itself in their minds.

It is no wonder then that they received full recognition of their rights in the Fundamental Rights Resolution passed at the Karachi Congress in 1933.

This proves that genuine redress of the grievances of women can only be realised when India becomes free and never within the framework of British Imperialism whose history is one unbroken chain of betrayals.

We are faced with almost similar handicaps when we turn to the social field where the women's organisations have mostly concentrated themselves. The Government has been utterly callous in the matter of social reform and education and without the two, national progress is greatly retarded. Let us take education.

There are people who still believe that it was Macaulay's famous minute that introduced education into India. As a matter of fact, it is his pernicious scheme to convert India into a nation of clerks that killed whatever education that already existed in the country. In fact, there was a regular network of schools in villages in those days which Imperialism ruthlessly destroyed, just as it crushed out Indian manufacturers, arts and handicrafts. In its place was introduced a hybrid education which was neither fish nor flesh. This system hit women the hardest. For, while men moved out into a new world and slowly absorbed the new tongue, women in their seclusion got entirely left in the dark. Their life grew gloomier and narrower and the breach between them and the men grew wider. And even now, when education is slowly percolating down, it has brought no joy or comfort.

Relegated to a position of little importance, education as a whole and of women in particular has suffered immensely in India. Apart from passing a series of acts from time to time, nothing has been done to make education a vital force in the life of the nation. It is the first item to be thrown overboard at times of financial stringency. The result is that the figures of literacy stand at 4 millions for women and 20 millions for men, out of a population of 353 million, a very flattering tribute to the Government! But nothing better can be expected of an administration when it can spare only 8% of the total national revenue for so important a cause. The total expenditure on education is 29 crores out of which 18 is spent from public funds and of this 2 ½ crores is spent on girls' education, 1 ½ crore being from public funds.

But even what little is done is so utterly useless. The vast bulk of the schools are single-teacher primary institutions and have been universally condemned as ineffective. Nor do the economic and social conditions permit the girl to take a course sufficient to ensure her permanent literacy. Out of 100 in class 1, barely 10 reach class IV and 5 class V, and six years is the period commonly prescribed for attaining permanent literacy. Thus the gain in literacy is depressingly poor and by no means commensurate with even the little expenditure. Except for private efforts, the State offers little opportunities for technical education for girls. Nor has this system any harmonious relation with the intimate everyday life of the people. It is like offering cold hard stones to the hungry ones who seek warm nourishing food.

Lack of educational facilities react on the social environment and vice versa. And it is due to want of proper education. The problem of child-marriage occupies a more prominent place in the social horizon, for, it is not only an evil in itself but brings a whole

17

multitude of miseries in its train, not the least of them being early maternity.

The figures for married girls are as follows per 1000 at the three age periods :—

| Age | 0-5 | 5-10 | 10—15 |
|---|---|---|---|
| Per 1000 | 30 | 193 | 381 |

This gives roughly a proportion of 43.7% of girls likely to be married below the age of 15.

The well-being of a nation is determined by sound healthy mothers. Hence the entire future of our nation is at stake here. It is not possible to get exact figures for maternity.

The Age of Consent Committee declared that about 42% of the girls were affected or likely to be, by early marriage. Roughly, the number of deaths in child-birth every year is calculated at 200,000. The figure is no doubt staggering and one which ought to sting us into sitting up with a gasp. But it is hardly to be wondered at under the conditions. Semi-starvation, malnutrition, entire absence of even the most ordinary amenities of life, lack of medical aid, these are some of the contributing factors. In fact, when we look round at the pitiable condition of our masses one is surprised the figure is not larger. But these figures hardly indicate the enormity of the damage. These reports pass silently over hundreds and thousands of young blossoming girls, wrecked for life physically and psychologically by forced premature motherhood. By all moral codes, it is rape but our social conscience is hard bound by dead old usages and the sharp edge of the dumb agony of these innocent victims penalised for life by cruel customs, hardly touches it. So the murders and rape go on, while we sit and gloat over the past glories of dead and gone Seetas and Savitris!

Associated with early maternity is another evil—frequent maternity. "An Indian woman oscillates between two states of gestation and lactation till death winds up the sorry tale," says an eminent Indian lady doctor. "One hundred out of every thousand girl-wives were doomed to die in child-birth."

Want of scientific aid leads to over 60% of fatalities in maternity and can be called by no other name but cold-blooded murder. But who heeds the cry of the poor helpless mother caught in the juggernaut wheels of imperialist exploitation and crude tradition?

Early marriage has many more and very far-reaching evil consequences apart from this physical disaster. It cuts short the period of childhood, deprives the girls of all the budding joys of girlhood such as free and romping life, snaps across their school-career shattering their intellectual growth, imposing responsibilities prematurely on their shoulders. Such severe handicaps necessarily undermine our society and retard its progress; and so completely does a wife pass into the potestas of her husband that a husband is the guardian of his minor wife and is entitled to insist on her living with him, however young she may be.

It is natural therefore that the All-India Women's Conference, the largest women's organization in India, should have decided at its first session to concentrate on these two items, educational reforms and prevention of child marriage. When Harbilas Sarda introduced his Child Marriage Bill in the Assembly, a vigorous campaign was carried on by women all over the country. And opposition came from conservative Hindus and Muslims alike. The Act however came into force on first April 1930 penalising marriage under fourteen for girls and eighteen for boys. But with it came disillusionment. The Act threatens to remain a dead letter unless it has both public backing as well as strong State enforcement. But under the present circumstances both are lacking and child marriages are taking place, particularly in rural areas where most people, have not even heard of the Sarda Act. An apathetic Government and the absence of public conscience, nullify and render ineffective the best of legislations.

The Women's Conference has fared no better in the field of educational demands. Apart from ceaseless representations to the various authorities, committees and boards dealing with this subject, nothing substantial has been achieved nor is likely to be, while political domination of India by an external force lasts.

# Purdah and Prostitute

It seems hardly credible to-day that only a century ago, widows were burnt in cold blood on their husband's funeral pyre. Even now the halo around sati lingers in our tradition-bound minds and we still entertain a lurking awe for them as heroic and holy women. Poor pitiful souls, helpless victims of the male savage egoistic passion! The so-called authority of Shastras coupled with the universal admiration which such acts of self-immolation awoke, created a hysterical fervour in the minds of these women. From early childhood, with their first lisp, they had learnt to stand in awe of man. The lot of those who are to-day saved from the devouring flames is hardly better. Their life is a living death being consumed by a slow fire of agony so far as the bourgeois class is concerned. Never having been taught to earn, uneducated, with no economic rights, they are dependent on man and at his mercy.

They are disfigured and relegated to a life of servility with scant regard for their feelings or notions. They are even regarded as objects of ill-omen. Remarriage is still looked upon with disfavour in spite of the Widow Remarriage Act of 1856.

Though conditions have been improving a little they are not as marked or appreciable as one would wish them to be. The existence of about two-and-half-crores of souls in agony, hardly reflects credit on those who are responsible for the well-being of the people in this country. Truly has some one remarked that the widow was lifted from the pyre but left in the cremation ground. In the lower middle-class many of these unhappy girls, helpless and desperate, fall easily into the wily meshes of traffickers in women. It is not uncommon to find them shut up in brothels in large cities or in places of pilgrimage. Whichever way they turn, theirs is a dark night of pain, unrelieved by even a single star.

Except for a few stray, though very creditable, efforts to ameliorate their condition, the Government does nothing to relieve their distress. The various institutions such as the Seva Sadans in Bombay and Madras presidencies, the Arya Samaj institutions all over Punjab, Saroj-Nalini Bharat Stree Mandal, etc. in Bengal are striving to serve these unhappy women, while the governments are cutting down even the few scholarships they used to give to widows. Under the present economic stress their conditions have considerably worsened and need some special care and attention on the part of society, since the State will not undertake any responsibility.

Purdah, another of the social evils, is also a remnant of medievalism and has no place or reality in the present-day world, as has been already pointed out. It is physical, economical and cultural loss to the nation to render a section of the society unproductive. This is greatly responsible for the low standard of living among the lower middle-class of Muslims. In a country where

Residents and Teachers of Women's Home of Service, Madras

people demand democracy, Purdah is an anachronism, for it denies the most elementary rights to citizens who are entitled to them. It stands in the way of education and of healthy physical growth, stultifies the mind and retards all development. Moreover it creates a harmful psychology in their progeny. Free, healthy, courageous citizens cannot be evolved out of dark seclusion. It makes women anaemic, neurotic and muscularly weak. Tuberculosis becomes rampant due to want of fresh air.

The present system of education fails to accelerate the pace of social progress. The 1% of the total revenue spent on public health is totally inadequate to ensure sound physical welfare. It is not surprising to find an increasing shortage of women in the 1931 report, maintaining a steady decline since 1901, though science is of opinion that the female child is better equipped than the male for survival and the proportion of women to men is most inadequate from the ages of 15 to 30—the reproductive age. This shows the low vitality of the women and their inadequate equipment to face motherhood. Tuberculosis is due not only to the bacilli but to overstrain as well, and has therefore become a permanent institution in this country.

Traffic in women and children is another of the problems which is engaging the attention of not only the women's organisations but even of the international bodies such as the League of Nations. But it is a thousand-headed octopus and cannot be treated as a single problem by a single measure. Unfortunately, the bourgeois mind still looks upon it as a sin that must be combated by religion and police.

Prostitution is essentially an economic question though

there are not many even in the women's movement to-day who share that view. At many of the women's conferences a great deal of stress is laid upon moral education and police vigilance. It shows a pitiable want of a grasp of fundamentals. That poverty is the cause in at least 80% of the cases, is shown by the enquiries made by the League of Nations in different countries. This is also the considered opinion of those connected with the Vigilance Associations in India. In industrial centres bad housing, unemployment, etc., add considerably to the problem. In addition to the ordinary prostitutes, there are others, Devadasis, girls dedicated to temples. With them too the question is partly economic and partly traditional. It is idle to think of dealing with this vast question through isolated efforts and a few private agencies.

It is the demand created by the leisured class that is responsible for the existence of prostitution and it is too deeply woven into the fabric of the society to be suppressed by piece-meal measures. It is the demand which creates the supply. So, it has to be treated at both ends. The Government machinery is ridiculously hopeless. A few Immoral Traffic Acts here and there do not even touch the fringe of the problem. Russia alone has tackled it intelligently and scientifically by attacking the very root of this evil not by regularising prostitution or merely shutting down brothels—the favourite method of all capitalist authorities—but by providing work, decent homes, a living wage, more humane conditions not only to those who are caught in the net but for all workers and potential prostitutes. That alone will solve the problem: the removal of the causes of poverty and the elimination of a privileged class.

In the field of legal demands the women's movement has been concentrating mostly on revision of marriage laws and removal of disabilities in the matter of inheritance.

Marriage and inheritance laws vary from religion to religion. Legally the Christian and the Muslim women are best off, except for a section of the women as in Punjab who observe customary laws. Although Islam permits polygamy, divorce to a certain extent should have counteracted the evil but for the traditional prejudice against divorce due to the "morality" created by the masculine dominance. It is the Hindu women who suffer more from faulty laws. The marriage laws need very drastic changes. Just now they are all one-sided and are nothing short of a cunning device to keep the women chained, with no hope of redress. Enforcement of monogamy with grant of divorce facilities are the general cry of the women and in this we find the Muslims also mingling their voices. But mere legal enactment will mean little unless the stigma attached to divorce is cleared away by a more rational attitude towards marriage than the prevailing superstitious one. A single moral code ensures far greater social purity than a double standard. Morality lies in a harmonious balance of forces and not in an unequal struggle.

# Workers and Wages

It has already been pointed out, that some of the demands which are put forth by the Women's organisation mostly reflect the needs of the bourgeois women, particularly in the matter of such social evils as Purdah, Polygamy, Divorce, etc. The working class is not so vitally affected by them. The women being themselves earners, are comparatively free from male thraldom, though social traditions do reduce them to a position inferior to that of men, socially as well as economically. As for the laws of inheritance, they do not affect even 50% of the women as they own no property.

It is to them that we have to turn to know the real India, dig deep into the earth and see wherein the true roots of the national misery lie. India is largely an agricultural country, or at least has been rendered so by imperialist design by the merciless destruction of Indian industries, not only of the small handicrafts but even of larger industries such as textile, ship-building, etc. The interests of British industries drove the industrial workers, now jobless and homeless, on to the villages creating an excessive pressure on land. In 1818 people dependent on land were only a little over 50%. But the latest figure stands at about 75%. It shows how, while every other country has gone on industrialising, India has been compelled into becoming more and more a cheap granary for supplying raw products to British industries, and a ready market for British manufacturers. Many of the jobless industrial workers who were forced on to the land, having no capital for investment, were reduced to labour for daily wages. And to-day very nearly half the agricultural population is landless, living on the verge of destitution, depending for its sole subsistence on agricultural labour, which is largely seasonal and uncertain. They are the most exploited part of the population economically and socially, being unorganised and thus the most hopeless.

As far as women are concerned they are rarely principle earners as ownership of land is mainly in male hands. But they provide labour in the fields. For every thousand labourers there are 457 women to 543 men. These figures hold good even for plantations. The average earnings of these labourers range between 2 to 4 annas according to the season. But as it is mostly paid in grain, the money value of it keeps changing as the price keeps varying. At the present rate, with a fall of nearly 50% no one gets more than 2 annas. But everywhere women are paid less—in some places about half of men's wages. This unjust system is part of the tradition handed down under masculine dominance. Masculine standard is the accepted one and according to that measure wages are fixed. That a woman-worker spends proportionately as much energy and labour and is entitled to the same wage is lost sight of. The same system is followed on the plantations also:—

|                              | Men            | Women        |
|------------------------------|----------------|--------------|
| Tea plantations in Assam     | Rs. 13  8  7   | Rs. 11  1  7 |
| Tea Plantations Sarma Valley | Rs. 10  13  0  | Rs. 8  6  1  |

per mensem.

Basic Rates of daily wages.

|                   | Men        | Women      |
|-------------------|------------|------------|
| Madras Presidency | Rs. 0-7-0  | Rs. 0-5-0  |
| Coorg             | 0-6-0      | 0-4-0      |

Let us now take the present proprietors. Their condition has been steadily deteriorating since the advent of the British rule, for, it is on them that the iron grip is strongest. It is out of the agriculturists that Imperialism squeezes the last drop out. The reasons for their impoverishment are many. Heavy taxation to maintain one of the most expensive administrations in the world, side by side with pressure on the land, leading to rapid fragmentation, uneconomic holdings, keeping down of the prices of agricultural commodities by manipulations of the exchange ratio, the interest on foreign obligations, complete absence of any state-help to intensify agriculture and improve live-stock by the introduction of modern scientific aids, lack of proper marketing facilities—these are but a few causes. Their income has slowly fallen and to-day it is barely over Rs. 20 per year, that is, less than an anna a day. Even before the phenomenal fall in prices, it did not go over 2 annas. This grinding poverty of so large and important a section of the population indicates an unhappy state of affairs for the nation. For, the peasants are practically the base of Indian economy and unless the average citizen has some margin for surplus produce and reasonable profit, the whole national economy keeps tottering on dangerous sands. Added to this is the staggering rural indebtedness which has attained the unbelievable figure of 1600 crores for the whole of India. There is little check on usury, the rates of interest being between 12—50% but rising up to even 75% and in some cases 100—300%. The impact of British rule on rural India can be gauged by the rapid rise of rural debt from 900 crores in 1929 to 1600 in 1936 almost doubled in 7 years. While the prices have fallen by 50% the taxes have been rising. In Madras they were raised by 181% in 1934 but finding their inability to collect taxes, the Government reduced them to 12%. That is how British Imperialism comes to the aid of the starving peasantry.

The lot of the tenants under semi-feudalistic lords, such as the Rajas, Zamindars, etc., is no better: if anything it is somewhat worse. They are no more than serfs in many cases. The present landlord system is a creation of British Imperialism by which the old tax-collectors and revenue farmers were made loyal adherents of Imperialism in India by investing them with full proprietary rights. Nearly one third of the land is under this system. Not only are the rents exorbitant, varying between 55—75% of the income, but in addition several other illegal exactions and secret rents are collected, driving the tenants to utter destitution. The tenants are helpless against this oppression, for the Government has fortified their allies through Tenancy Laws which vest the landlords with very extensive powers against the tenantry. And in any struggle between the two, the authorities always side with the vested interests however just the grievances of the poor toilers may be.

This shows that the problem of rural India and its poverty are so interlinked with the existence of British rule in India and political factors so fundamentally closed up with it, that any half-measure of reform would prove abortive and superficial.

Although famines and floods, are as annual as seasons themselves, there is no provision to protect the people from these devastations. Irrigation is slow and costly and is designed more to benefit the British manufacturers than to help Indian cultivators.

Now let us turn to Industrial India and see what its condition is under the present regime. The 1931 census gives the figure at 26,000,000 for industrial labour.

The poor condition of the industries coupled with world depression serves to keep the standard of living of the labourers low. The hours of work are still too high for a tropical country and for a people impoverished in every way. The housing is bad and inadequate as the Industrial Commission testifies:—"The worst type of chawl consists of single rooms, pitch dark and possessing very little in the way of windows... the floors are damp... the courtyard receives insufficient sun and air... and most insanitary smell hangs about the place." The Whitley Commission remarks :—"The areas occupied by the working class present pictures of terrible squalor... resulting evils are physical deterioration, high infant mortality and a general high death rate." Probably the majority of factory-owners make no endeavour to mitigate the discomfort, to use a mild word, that the hot weather brings to their operatives. About 97% of the labourers live in single rooms—that is, on an average 6 to 9 persons occupy one room. It is no wonder that infant mortality reaches the staggering figure of 825.5 per 1000 in some of the areas.

The wages paid are most inadequate and under the cry

of depression they are being still lowered. Under these conditions it is no wonder that the money-lender figures just as much in these areas as in the rural. The industrial workers are as much enslaved as the agricultural.

Legislation does not adequately protect children even in organized industries. Mr. Gangully says in his book: "In the carpet factories of Amritsar, children ranging between 9 and 14 are made to work through 11 hours a day for 2 annas." The Whitley Commission remarks "It was clear from the evidence that these children were in the position of being obliged to work any number of hours required by their masters."

The rising unemployment has increased the distress amongst them and the complete absence of any social insurance leaves them absolutely destitute.

So far as the bulk of women-workers is concerned, they are mostly in factories, their number being gradually reduced in mines, and a few being employed in transport. Taking the figures from 1929 we find a steady decline in their number from 257,161 to 225,632. It is no doubt mainly due to the depression and increasing unemployment but also because of the employers' preference for men-labour to avoid the "inconvenient" provisions relating to women, such as maternity benefits, prohibition of night shifts, etc. Greater mechanisation and haphazard legislation have considerably added to the difficulties of the women workers. For instance, the principle of prohibiting women from under-ground mining work, has worked havoc amongst the mining families, by too rapid elimination and lack of substitute employment. Hundreds of women have been lifted out of the industry and simply left to starve in the most callous manner.

# Labour and Motherhood

The Provisions of the Indian Factories Act protecting women from excessive work are neither satisfactory nor effective. But the sheer mockery of it is evidenced when we find that even within this modest measure not more than 10% of the actual working women can be brought. Maternity benefits, medical aid, welfare service, creches, are made available to only a small fraction of the women-workers. As it is mostly of a voluntary nature, it enables employers to escape responsibility in the absence of enforcing legislation.

The greater bulk of them are illiterate and no attempt is made to bring any light to their dark minds. Nor are educational facilities provided for their children. And we have the pitiable spectacle of neglected children roaming the streets, aimless, uncared, undirected, deteriorating, falling easy prey to mischief and crime. How many of our high-browed sisters, who talk so patronisingly with pious airs of the crimes amongst working-class families, see their own hands stained with criminal neglect in it? On its material side, lack of education means inefficiency and poorer production and hence a loss to national revenue.

All female labour is regarded as unskilled and the

principle of discrimination is applied. The women are paid even less than unskilled male labour. In reality this custom of underpayment on the ground of sex overshadows many of the other grievances. It is not only unjust but very humiliating. The following table is illuminating as well as perplexingly pathetic.

Average daily earnings.

|  | Men | Women |
|---|---|---|
| Bombay | Rs. 1 8 0 | Rs. 0 11 11 |
| Ahmedabad | 1 6 8 | 0 12 6 |
| Sholapur | 1 0 4 | 0 6 8 |

Here we see an enormous difference in the earnings of women as compared with that of men in the three centres of Bombay Presidency in the same industry. It is half in Bombay, in Ahmedabad it is a little more than half and in Sholapur less than half. Are we to believe that efficiency varies in this absurd fashion? In the jute industry of Bengal the average earnings per month of a man varies from Rs. 11 to 40 whereas that of a woman never goes beyond Rs. 15.

| Mineral Field | UNDERGROUND | | | SURFACE | | |
|---|---|---|---|---|---|---|
|  | Skilled | Un-skilled | Women | Skilled | Un-skilled | Women |
| Bihar & Orissa (Coal) | 0 12 9 | 0 9 9 | 0 8 6 | 0 13 3 | 0 8 9 | 0 6 9 |
| Bengal (Coal) | 0 12 3 | 0 9 0 | 0 7 6 | 0 11 6 | 0 8 6 | 0 6 0 |
| Central Provinces (Manganese) | 1 0 6 | 0 7 0 | 0 4 0 | 1 0 9 | 0 8 0 | 0 4 9 |
| Punjab (Salt) | 1 1 3 | 1 10 9 | 0 9 9 | 1 1 3 | 0 13 3 | 0 6 0 |

These figures are for 1929.

Another factor which greatly affects the women workers is the system of indirect employment or dependent labour as it is called, that is to say, they receive wages through a principal worker. A far larger number of women than men come under this system. Out of every 1000 such dependent workers 733 are women. This constitutes a fruitful field for exploitation and cries for immediate abolishment.

In all domestic service too, women are at a disadvantage in the matter of wages. And nowhere can they expect redress and get the principle of equal wages established unless this male-dominated society is changed to one founded on equal opportunities and equal rights.

This is the dark and sorry tale of nearly 90% of the women in India. The bourgeois leaders of the feminist movement would do well to remember that what these weary hunger-stricken women cry for is not the right to work but the "Right to the gains of their labour." The legal rights of inheritance touch them not. They inherit but sorrow and pain from generation to generation. They are the producers of the wealth but they remain beggars. They have with their sweated labour built up the properties which a small handful of women are seeking to possess. Such demands within the present economic framework only means securing privileges for one class at the expense of another, and the right to exploit the large masses of women along with men. Economic freedom in its genuine sense can become a reality only when there is a more scientific and sane system of production and distribution and the forces of economic progress are consciously directed towards the good of all.

One other demand the women in India are seeking to

assert as their inherent right is the right to motherhood. It is as old as womanhood itself. We know that even among the primitives, women sought to restrict or make selective their progeny through a variety of methods, most of them being no doubt very crude. Things are not very much better to-day in spite of greater knowledge of science. Social prejudice against birth control is almost savage in its ferocity. Severe penalties are imposed upon those who disseminate such knowledge. The reason is two-fold. The masculine-dominated society always stresses the importance of women as a breeder. Economically and politically, men are useful as toilers, as soldiers, to be exploited to keep a small class in luxury and idle parasitic existence. All Imperialistic minded rulers encourage large families. One of the old relics of early Aryan days, when men were needed for conquest, is the usual form of blessing an Indian woman with "may you be blest with eight sons." For the more the ambition for military and Imperialist glory, the greater the effort to encourage breeding and the greater the enslavement of women. The other reason is because women freed from the penalty of undesired motherhood will deal a death blow to man's vested interest in her. He can no more chain and enslave her through children. And therefore this war which woman is waging to-day against man, against society, against nature itself, is against her sexual dependence. For as long as women cannot control their bodies and escape the sentence that nature seems to have decreed upon them, their social and economic freedom would be innocuous. It is for the same reason that man strives desperately to thwart her efforts through religious canons, legal statutes and social codes.

Birth control has both a moral as well as a material aspect to it. Woman feels that motherhood is too sacred and responsible a function to be left to the exigencies of accidental circumstances, or to be determined by ignorance. It must be undertaken by a full realisation of its joy and responsibility, controlled and regulated according to the emotional urge and physical capacity of the woman. For this purpose, sound knowledge of sex, birth control and the use of contraceptives is essential. As Margaret Sanger puts it in her own inimitable way: "The sex life of women has been clouded in darkness, restricted, repressive and morbid. Women have not had the opportunity to know themselves or to give play to their inner natures that they might create a morality, practical and idealistic, for their own needs. She must know the power of the sex force, its use and its abuse, and how to direct it for the benefit of the race. Then she can transmit to her children an equipment that will enable them to break the bonds that have held humanity enslaved for ages. Abused soil brings forth stunted growths. An abused motherhood has brought forth a low order of humanity."

Few had stressed, before the rise of the women's movement, the immorality of the "Property Rights" of man over woman's body. But the new crusaders in the cause of women's rights are destroying that dead hand which would reach out to extinguish the flame of a new women, a new Social order and a morality. From the point of national benefit, the need of birth control is keenly felt, both for economic and eugenic reasons. Though a heavy population is not the cause of poverty, it adds considerably to the burden of the poor. And though the opponents of birth control may choose to close their eyes to glaring ugly facts, the truth is that a large number of women of the working-class resort to birth control and in the absence of scientific knowledge come to grave grief by the use of crude and unhealthy measures.

While the high-browed virtuous middle-class men shut out useful scientific knowledge which would economically and eugenically help the large masses of workers and save them from desperate means for restriction, the equally virtuous women of this self same bourgeoisie obtain behind barred doors all the help and relief which science can give but money alone can provide.

Birth control is not curtailing births but scientifically regulating them. To have a clean and healthy nation, indiscriminate reproduction has to be avoided. All congenital diseases can be minimised greatly through selective breeding. And as for venereal disease which is eating into the vitals of nearly 47% of the people in India, it cannot be brought under control without the help of birth control to aid medical measures.

The future of the women of India lies with those 90% who toil and labour in green fields and dark factories and the extent of consciousness that can be roused in them to the rights of their sex, the measure of the power and influence they wield will be determined by the strength of the class they belong to. Those who would will freedom for women, vindicate their rights and give them perfect equality, must work for the larger freedom of the exploited and the oppressed and wipe out the society which keeps the few in luxury at the expense of the many. The women's problem is the human problem and not merely a sex problem. It is not liberty or franchise that will fundamentally change their position to their advantage but the change of the basis and entire framework of society. We have the two striking examples of Italy and Germany on the one hand and Soviet Russia on the other, for, while in the latter the women are establishing complete equality, in the former they are losing even their few hard won rights. India, if she is to have an emancipated womanhood, must look to a revolutionised future, when class-conflict shall have faded away as a dim far-off memory, poverty shall have been wiped out, and woman shall have obtained not only her sex-rights but man and woman together shall have won their human rights as well to live as dignified human individuals.

# Imperialism & Class Struggle

The birth of the Socialist Party in the Congress marks an important epoch in Indian politics, though few perhaps have realised its significant role. People in their ignorance merely regard it as a symbol of revolt against Gandhiji and Gandhism, an indiscriminate importation of inassimilative western notions. There are some who are sympathetic, but regard its appearance as premature. All these betray a lack of historical knowledge and historical sense. The majority takes its stand on the ground that our struggle to-day is against a foreign power and the talk of class-war confuses the issue and gives rise to internecine fights. This shows that a great many people have not understood the nature of Imperialism or the characteristics which a struggle against it ought to develop. Unless we get a clear understanding on that, it is not possible to get a correct perspective of India's struggle or of the role of the Socialist Party in it.

Imperialism is the outcome of capitalistic production, that is, production of commodities sold at the highest profit; hence its need for a constant expansion of market to maintain a level of prosperity. It also means export of capital from an industrialised country to undeveloped tracts, thus reaping heavy dividends. Such capital is employed not in industrial development, for that would necessarily mean limiting the imports coming from the "Home" market. So it goes into the development of the means of transportation. And so far as the exports go, the expansion is only illusory. No real expansion is possible unless production also increases and this is not possible except through improved means of production, which again has no chance in a colonial country. So, the high rate of profit that the foreign creditor derives from investments in colonies is raised by the continuous exploitation of the masses by depriving them of even the little surplus they might otherwise have saved. Thus the heavy taxation in India represents the high interest rate paid to the foreign creditor.

Now let us examine the relationship between this Imperialism and its Indian allies, such as the princes, landlords capitalists, middlemen, money-lenders, etc., for, then we shall have realised the class basis of the Indian anti-Imperialist struggle. For the efficient working of Imperialism an Indian agency is indispensable, because without some such social basis it would not be possible for it to maintain its hold. The landlords, the capitalists, the middlemen in India are the creation of Imperialism. When the East India Company came in, they found a country where the old order was passing away, but trade had already become an important social factor, though the industry was of pre-capitalist mode. This was a stumbling block in the path of a free importation of cheap manufacture for which a ready market had to be created somehow. So the handicrafts were ruthlessly destroyed, throwing hundreds of thousands out of employment and abruptly converting the country into a purely agricultural one. This was also in the interest of Imperialism, for the "Home" country had to be assured of an unlimited supply of raw material for its factories.

Left to itself the social process of evolution from semi-feudalistic society and pre-capitalistic industry would have worked itself out as in other countries. The decaying feudalistic order would have been destroyed by the rising bourgeois and industry would have passed into the capitalist mould. Instead, the foreign intervention brought in a chain of events entirely different in character. The old feudalistic absolutism was overthrown as a political power and in its place a whole lot of tax-farmers was created from among the contractors, the highest bidders being made the overlords of several villages and invested with full proprietary powers, over and above the keeping of puppet princes. They were to be the "pillars of Imperialism" in India. The pre-capitalistic form of production was also maintained as its retention as an integral part of colonial capitalism prevents the rise of mass prosperity which must necessarily bring in its wake industrialisation. Here we begin to see the link between Imperialism and this ballast of feudal conditions and why it is impossible to overcome the one without overcoming the other.

Let us now understand this semi-feudalistic condition which Imperialism maintains as its handmaid. About 75 per cent or about 260 millions of the Indian population live on agriculture. Of these nearly 12 millions live on the rents they receive as landlords or ruling chiefs, their income being estimated at nearly 180 crores. This class leads the typical parasitical existence living on an unearned income. Nor is this income spent for productive purposes. It is mostly diverted to urban areas, squandered on degenerate luxuries or spent abroad. The rural areas are left starving for finances for general improvement and the same is the fate of industries. Nearly one-third of the cultivated area is owned by this class and all this vast tract of land and the millions that toil on it are doomed to a dark gloomy existence.

The rest of the land is owned by the Government. The fate of these areas and of those who cultivate them is hardly any better, though they are formally free from feudal bondage. All agriculturists, whether they be petty land proprietors or tenants, are practically a proletarianised mass, for, they do not in either case possess the land they work upon. They are completely at the mercy of the land-owner. The living they eke out is more in the nature of wages than an independent income. In addition there is the money-lender to whom their produce is mortgaged.

The intense overcrowding on the lands due to the absence of industries to absorb the surplus population now struggling on the land, the primitive methods of production which do not give India a chance of competing in the world-market and merely making the life of the villager an unrelieved drudgery, all these are accountable for the utter pauperisation of the peasantry. This continuous exploitation, frustration of every effort, a futureless horizon, have killed the incentive in them, filling them with a despairing fatalism.

The solution of the agrarian problem is, therefore, an essential condition for India getting out of this vicious rut. It alone will lead to successful industrialisation which must necessarily lead to the general prosperity. This will relieve the pressure on the land, raise the purchasing power of the masses and give India a place in the world-market. But, to bring this about, a radical change in the social structure is essential. If antiquated modes have to be replaced by newer and more scientific ones, the feudalistic system must give place to a more just and equitable system of land tenure, the pre-capitalistic mode of production to mechanisation, then surely the overthrow of Imperialism must also mean the abolition of landlordism. This will release the peasantry from its present economic slavery and open up the land for intense cultivation by modern methods and all the wealth which now runs into unproductive channels will be available for fostering industries. This will mean great stimulation of the general economic life of the country.

Lastly, there are the middlemen who are also partners in this Imperialistic game of exploitation. In the absence of any sound credit system, usury offers an attractive opening. In the absence of any marketing facilities the middlemen plunder the poor peasantry. Thus, under the pre-capitalistic mode of production, the middlemen have a good stake and they will not be a willing party to the abolition of this system of economy which is the inevitable prelude to normal industrialisation. Now the question may be raised why this historic task of abolishing the feudalistic system cannot be done by the bourgeois in India as has been the case in most other countries. For the obvious reason that the Indian masses today are in reality the slaves of capitalism, for Imperialism is the ultimate phase of capitalism, the semi-feudal conditions are maintained by Imperialism as part of its function.

The Indian bourgeois is, therefore, an instrument of capitalism in the exploitation of the masses. Imperialism has buttressed itself behind the upper classes. Whenever a peasant struggles against excess rent or tax, a worker to better his condition of living, or the subjects of the native states resist the absolute powers of the Princes, the Imperialist forces appear as protectors of the exploiters. Thus, when the toiling masses who form nearly 90 per cent of the population fight for complete national independence they must necessarily fight Imperialism in all its strength, that is, together with all its allies.

Indian capitalism has grown as a by-product of Imperialism and is linked up with Imperialist trade and industry. Due to its own contradictions, British Imperialism, though unwillingly, is forced to give some economic and political concessions to Indian capitalism and other upper classes to maintain themselves and allow them to grow, though the normal development is chequered. The capitalist class is more than satisfied with its condition. Its existence is therefore, conditioned by the continuance of Imperialism, whereas by the overthrow of Imperialism its life is endangered. Under the frame-work of Imperialism whatever political reforms are granted, the condition of the masses cannot improve. In fact, by the new constitution or any similar reform, the alliance between Imperialism and the Indian bourgeois will be tightened, leading to greater exploitation of the toiling classes. The classes that will fight Imperialism are those whose condition will deteriorate by the presence of Imperialism. It is only those classes who have "nothing to lose but their chains and a world to gain" that will fight—and these are the workers, the peasants and the lower middle classes.

In a colonial country, class-struggle inevitably coincides with the struggle for national freedom, for the anti-Imperialist movement is also a struggle against capitalism and landlordism. The same arguments apply to Indian conditions. The Indian capitalist will throw in his lot with the national struggle in so far as his interests conflict with those of foreign capitalism. But with the concession of facilities to improve and develop his capitalist investment in indigenous industrialism, he automatically turns into co-partnership with the very force against which he was ranged in opposition only a little while ago. Both draw upon cheap Indian labour and cheap raw material. It pays capitalism, whether white or coloured, to keep native labour at a low ebb.

The post-war chaos that capitalism had to face, induced British Imperialism to change its colonial policy. The purchasing power of the Indian peasants being at a very low par, some effort had to be made to raise the standard of living in order to stimulate trade. So, a limited scheme of industrialisation was launched upon and high tariffs set up. This meant a renewed field for investment and the sale of heavy machinery and a demand for engineering experts, all for the benefit of the foreign creditor, and the "Home" country and the Indian bourgeois, all ready instruments in working out this scheme of a more direct exploitation of the Indian masses. For this would mean larger surplus value of a big dividend to the share-holders. The Indian capitalist was to be lavishly fed on high tariffs to meet the budget deficits. But in this declining stage of capitalism its last desperate effort to reinstate itself is failing. While the prices of finished goods rise, thanks to the tariffs, the price of the raw material falls and the purchasing power of the masses goes down bringing in its wake greater chaos. The acute distress caused by this is creating a spirit of revolt in the masses which is leading to a closer union between the British and Indian capitalist. To retain this support British Imperialism is launching upon political reform, a few make-believe concessions that only mean the strengthening of the chains. For, without an appreciable expansion in the productivity of labour, the Indian capitalist can only profit by further exploitation of the Indian proletariat and that is what we are witnessing to-day.

The crisis created by the contradiction of Imperialism cannot be overcome unless by the termination of Imperialism. Thus alone can India save herself from destruction. Reformism cannot find a foothold under present conditions. It has a place only under capitalist prosperity when concessions could still be wrung from it. Normal social, economic and political growth being impossible under these circumstances, because, they are inherent in a colonial system, the system itself needs to be changed. The progressive undermined state of national economy means progressive contraction of the purchasing power of the masses. An expanding market is the basic condition for industrial development. And this is impossible with a declining purchasing power. Hence, even though there is plenty of labour power going waste, there cannot be industrial progress. Our internal market can expand only when the Indian peasant is spared a little of his surplus produce instead of being wiped clean by rents, taxes— direct or indirect—and usurious interest. This is not possible in the present property relations within the framework of Imperialism. The present state is an expression of Imperialist domination. The radical changes it needs to undergo before any appreciable benefit can be derived, cannot be effected by Indianisation of services, responsibility at the centre, or fiscal autonomy. That would only mean drawing a larger Indian element into the vortex of the Imperialist machinery and the Indian bourgeois being given a junior partnership in the business. The power will still remain in the hands of a small minority and not transferred to the people and the old game of exploitation will continue.

In order to mobilise and harness the mass energy to the anti-imperialist struggle there must be political consciousness in the masses. This is possible only through the economic fight built out of demands for a few immediate items. The economic motive is one of the strongest in the human element and it is through the economic demands that a programme that they can visualise as freedom can be built up and out of this struggle will rise the great struggle for political power by the masses. Roughly these demands will work out as follows:—

1. Higher wages and better conditions of labour;
2. 40 hours 1 week;
3. Insurance against unemployment, sickness, old age and adequate protection for women workers during maternity;
4. 50 per cent reduction in rent;
5. Annulment of the indebtedness of the peasants, workers and artisans;
6. Complete exemption of rent of uneconomic holdings;
7. Control of usury;

8.  Abolition of all indirect taxes;
9.  Free and compulsory primary education; and
10. Freedom of press, platform and association.

In the course of their struggle for these concessions they will learn by experience that even the few crumbs have ceased to fall from the Imperialist table, and the solution as well as the salvation lies in a radical change of the entire system. And the struggle on their immediate demands will develop into the struggle for political power. It is after the realisation of this struggle that the National Constituent Assembly comes into being. We thus find that the composition of the Constituent Assembly is determined by the class-basis of the national movement and the constitution by the social composition of the Constituent Assembly. The talk of convoking it at this stage with the sanction of Imperialism is sheer delusion. It would be anything but a Constituent Assembly. In fact, it will be a positive danger, for under the name of Constituent Assembly, a puppet of Imperialism will come into being to lead to further strengthening of its domination. Moreover, it will lack both the mass sanction and composition. An analysis of the nature and function of Imperialism and the anti-imperialist struggle, the reasons for the rise of the Socialist party, answer themselves. The Indian struggle is unique in its own way. Historically, it ought to be democratic, but in view of the world-conditions, the decaying condition of capitalism and the class-basis of the entire structure, it assumes the features of a socialistic struggle.

It is stupid for people to imagine that class-struggle is a creation of the socialists. Class-struggle is a historical fact. It has existed from the time primitive communist society ceased to be. One may ban the use of the term "Class struggle" as the word "Sex" was tabooed in the 19th century. But from merely abstaining from mentioning a fact, the fact does not cease to be. As long as the means of production remain in the hands of the few, labour remains a commodity for exchange which the owner of the productive machinery converts into huge profits for himself, as under capitalism and feudalism. Under modern capitalism production is socialised. Labour is collectively performed and is an indivisible unit. But the means of this production—land, factories, mines, railways, banks, ships, etc.—are owned by a mere handful who have nothing to do with actual production. The minimum human requirements are not satisfied; millions starve, hence the obvious conflicts between the two classes, owners and the toilers. This contradiction can be overcome only when collective ownership of the means of production is established, that is, when the producers also become the owners of the means of production.

In conclusion, I wish to impress upon you the necessity of rallying round the Congress and making it the chief organ of the anti-imperialist struggle. There are historical reasons why the Congress should be the real anti-imperialist platform. Ever since 1921, it is the only organisation which has been fighting imperialism. No doubt, the leadership is either bourgeois or the people who have the bourgeois ideology. It represents however the objective strivings of the masses, that is, freedom from foreign domination, and the politically conscious people are in the Congress. The content of the Congress is not bourgeois. Therefore to create any petty-bourgeois anti-imperialist platform outside the Congress and to try to duplicate it would be wrong. It will become the sham replica of a Working Class Party and cannot embrace the entire petty-bourgeois anti-imperialists. All class-conscious working-class elements and the true anti-imperialists, rather than running away from the Congress, calling it bourgeois, should in fact enter it and clarify the issue of the masses, placing before them the correct programme so that the class differentiation that is taking place in the country may be reflected inside the Congress. Then alone shall we be able to capture the Congress movement and prevent the leadership from converting it into a bourgeois party, thus stealing from us the Congress heritage.

I

Towards Progress
& Freedom

By Mrs. Margaret Cousins.

II

Art in Early Indian Life

By Mrs. Sakuntala Thampi.

III

A Short Sketch of

Maharani Shree Jijabai Bhonsale

By H. H. Maharani Indirabai Holkar of Indore.

IV

Women's Disabilities in Law

By Shyam Kumari Nehru.

V

Indian Indigenous Industries

By Mrs. Jayashriben Raiji.

Mrs. Margaret E. Cousins

# Towards Progress & Freedom

By Margaret E. Cousins, B. Mus

In 1900 A. D. the condition of Indian womanhood in general was at its lowest ebb. In 1939 A. D. the tide of political, educational, and social honour for women has risen so high that India has 80 (eighty) women Members in its Legislatures of Provinces and States, and thus ranks third amongst the nations of the world as regards the political influence and position secured by its women— the United States of America and Russia being first and second respectively.

How has this leap from the depths to the heights been made in forty years? And in a country where change has been proverbially slow?

Primarily it is because the movement for the progress and freedom of the women of India is one and the same movement as that for the progress and freedom of India itself. In that sense Indian men and women march together and efforts to improve conditions as individuals, communities, sexes, classes are related at every point with the most urgent need of any subject-country, that of its restoration to political independence.

In Vedic times (say, 3000 years ago), women had freedom of movement, education, religious rights, equal opportunities with the men of those far-off times, as is found in the internal evidence of the literature of that era. This freedom was curtailed in the succeeding Brahminical era. Again, the Reformation produced by the teaching of the Buddha set men and women on a new path of freedom and women took their place in the religious, social, educational and administrative spheres of the national life as free individuals and citizens. This is proved by historical documents, accounts of educational institutions, orders of Buddhist nuns as well as monks, the beautiful sweetness of freedom of men and women in family relationships as portrayed by the paintings, sculptures and stories of that thousand years of Indian history. Alas, that tide of good life also ebbed, and with the invasions of foreigners, and the internal ambitions and wars of neighbouring Rulers, freedom again decayed, and, as always in times of militarism, women suffered the greatest defeat, and became the most suppressed section of an exhausted, cowed, subservient people.

Arising out of the practically uniform system of education imposed on India by the British, the generation of students in 1900 showed some result in awakened national consciousness. This education, though faulty, had made for unity. It had given girls the same quality of education as boys, though then and even still it provided finance and facilities for only one-sixth the number of girls compared with boys. Thus in the early years of this century Indian women had taken a stride towards high grade education and this has increased notably so that now Indian women are medical Doctors, Barristers,

Insertion of Mrs. M. E. Cousins as first woman Honorary Magistrate in India. Madras, February 1923

Lawyers, Professors of all subjects, Honorary Magistrates, one, the Surgeon-General of an Indian State, another, a District Munsiff whose next promotion will be to become the first woman Judge. Thousands of women are professors and teachers, nurses, and artistes in painting, music, dancing and film work. Educationally the tide is rising for the Indian people, but oh, how slowly in view of the figures of mere literacy in their own mother-tongue— only 2.9 per cent of women literate and 14% of men, and the total expenditure on Education is only 8% of the national revenues. There undoubtedly still exists in the country a deep-rooted apathy and opposition against girls being educated. A case in point is the large ancient city of Kumbakonam in Tamil country where the Municipality has enforced compulsory education for boys for the last seventeen years, but not applied it in a single ward to girls, though they have amassed a surplus fund of Rs. 45,000!

Those women who received education have done credit to their sex and have led the movements for social reforms such as legislation to prevent Child Marriages, to terminate the Devadasi system (temple dancing girls) to get more just inheritance rights for women and equal pay for equal work. From 1912 there began the movement for creating Associations of Women. This was the foundation of group-consciousness and united action which has been an undoubted factor in bringing about the speed of the emergence of India's womanhood into power and publicity. The Bharat Stree Mandal, the Poona Seva Sadan, the Women's Indian Association, the Young Women's Christian Association, the Sarojini Dutt Mahila Samaj, the Women's Brahmo Samaj work and many other large provincial and community groups were rousing the women of the educated classes to think and act for their own improvement as a dedicated part of their aspiration for national freedom. For instance, the first object of the Women's Indian Association was, "To present to Women their responsibilities as daughters of India; as wives and mothers they have the task of training, guiding and forming the character of the future rulers of India." This was the keynote of the afternoon adult classes and lectures in many subjects which, combined with the promotion of recreation clubs and social service projects, made women ready between 1900 and 1919 to request that when political reforms were instituted, women should have in them the same status and responsibilities as citizens as their menfolk. This occurred in the historic Women's Deputation to the Hon. E. S. Montagu, then Indian Secretary of State, and its result was the enfranchisement of women in the Montagu-Chelmford Reforms on the same terms as men by each Provincial Legislative Council, starting with the Madras Presidency in 1921.

The propaganda for Woman Suffrage was carried on chiefly by the Women's Indian Association which also supported the propaganda of the Indian Home Rule League, though it maintained a non-party independence. The fact that two women, Dr. Annie Besant and Srimati Sarojini Naidu, were Presidents of the Indian National Congress in 1917 and 1921 respectively, and that the former was interned in 1916 for upholding free speech and free association in the cause of Indian Home Rule, did much to stimulate women in desiring their own enfranchisement and in the agitation for political freedom. The men of the country also willingly then supported the women's claim to citizenship and availed themselves of women's desire for "the same opportunities of service" to their country as men possessed, small though they then were.

It thus happened that within the short period of ten years (1917-27) women in India claimed and were granted the political vote, a couple of years later used it for the first time, within the next three years, were granted the right to be nominated or elected to the Legislatures, and in 1927 one woman Dr. Muthulakshmi Reddi was unanimously elected by the members of the Council to be its Deputy Speaker, a world record. Throughout the country women were by then also members of Legislative and Municipal Councils to the extent of several hundreds though till then no woman had been elected to the Legislative Council. Several including Srimati Kamaladevi had contested elections with men candidates, but had been defeated.

In 1926 the organisation of the All-India Women's Conference, concentrated and unified, awakened women in all parts of India, and at its first session in Jan. 1927 in Poona under the Presidency of H. H. the Maharani of Baroda a new drive began for improved education, especially of girls, and arising out of it followed an organised attack on Child-Marriage and its attendant evils of Child Widowhood, and immature parentage. This organisation now holds the premier place as the voice and instrument of Indian womanhood on public affairs, educational, economic, legal, social, and political. Much of its success and growth in popularity is due to the organising ability and self-sacrificing hard work put

Standing Committee of the All-India Women's Conference, Bombay, 1930
Front Row: Left to Right

Mrs. Hamid Ali, Mrs. Brijlal Nehru, Mrs. P. K. Sen, Mrs. Kamaladevi Chattophadyay, Mrs. Sarojini Naidu,
Mrs. Hindekoper, Mrs. Rustomji Faridoonji, Mrs. Cousins, Mrs. Hamsa Mehta

into it by Srimati Kamaladevi who was its organising Secretary during its second, third and fourth years, and who guided the formation of its constitution and established constituencies in 30 areas by her strenuous touring.

When Civil Disobedience brought about the Round Table Conferences, this All-India Women's Conference which agitated for women representatives at these Conferences and voiced women's demands that there should be joint electorates, not communal electorates, no reserved or nominated seats for women, that literacy should be a qualification for women voters, and that mere wifehood of a man-voter should not be a qualification. They also called for an increased percentage of voting power for woman in the new India Bill then being drafted, and the removal of sex disabilities for taking Office. Those who most directly brought about the present political status of women in India through their personal contact with the members of the British Parliament were (chronologically) Dr. Annie Besant, Mrs. Sarojini Naidu, Mrs. and Miss Tata, Mrs. Subbarayan, Dr. Muthulakshmi Reddi, Rajkumari Amrit Kaur, Mrs. Hamid Ali.

All these years the tide of patriotism was rising throughout the masses of the Indian people and reached a climax when in 1929 Gandhiji started Satyagraha.

The response of the women to the call for sacrifice from the day when the Mahatma started the Dandi March in defiance of the Salt Law was magnificent. Within the next three years, over five thousand women had served terms of severe imprisonment, they had suffered from lathi charges, from cruelty, loss of property, loss of livelihood, from ill-health, loss of caste, loss of reputation. They willingly faced publicity of the most trying kind in picketing drink shops and foreign cloth shops, in walking in public processions, in proceedings in law courts. They sacrificed all kinds of cherished privileges of caste, ceremonial purity, and privacy. The Cause of Swaraj swept all taboos and customs before it. The revered leader Gandhiji was sufficient guarantee of the righteousness of whatever new actions had to be taken. In struggling for the country's freedom women achieved their own freedom to an extent hardly credible. In the great crusade between 1929 and 1933 women of all castes, communities, all degrees of poverty and wealth shared the burdens, the pain, the sacrifices, the joys, and the individual new freedom of acting in response to the need of the moment without reference to old precedents, customs, shibboleths of "proper" sex-conduct and sex separateness. Men and Women acted as souls, not as sexes, and soul-force was their weapon. They learnt new respect for one another's all-round capacities and characters displayed in that new light of nationalism. Srimati Sarojini Naidu was the most outstanding woman of those years and Srimati Kamala Devi was the leader of the youth in them, her beauty, eloquence, brains, audacity and charm making her particularly popular. Like many others she almost ruined her health in those days of dark repression. Other prominent women leaders were Mrs. Rukmini Lakshmipathi, Mrs. Hamsa Mehta, Mrs. Zutshi, Dr. Muthulakshmi Reddi, Mrs. Nellie Sen Gupta, Satyavati Devi, Mrs. Captain, Miraben (Miss Slade), Mrs. Jaffar Ali, Durgabai, Kuttimala Amma.

Having been to the prisons, the next wave of the tide in the affairs of Indian women took them to the polls. In the General Election of February, 1937, the women voters (about five million) were so enthusiastic in electioneering and casting their vote for Congress that it was evident that the women of the masses, the women workers in villages and towns were awake to their responsibilities and their powers as enfranchised citizens using the vote as a direct means of securing self-government. Though disliking the reservation of a certain number of seats for contest between women candidates only, yet women used their votes to ensure that the Congress women should be elected. In areas where women contested seats with men the Congress women candidates were extraordinarily successful. One woman elementary teacher defeated the Vice-Chancellor of the University of her Province, another the simple little wife of a Doctor, routed the President of a District Board who had been the Parliamentary Member of that place for twelve years. It was the combination of Congress and woman (voters wanting to show their gratitude to womanhood for their sacrifices for patriotism) that put women at the head of the polls.

To-day amongst the eighty-odd women who are legislators one is a Minister with the portfolio of Local Self-Government and Public Health—Mrs Vijialakshmi Pandit, sister of Jawaharlal Nehru—one is Deputy President of an Upper Legislative House, three are Deputy Speakers of Legislative Assemblies, four are Parliamentary Secretaries, several are Party Whips. While amongst these women are Hindus, Muhammadans, Parsees, Indian Christians, Sikhs, there is a noticeable absence of any communal feeling. There is a beautiful unity amongst the Indian women in public life and this and their belief in non-violence as the technique of future struggles will ensure their valuable continuance and unique contribution in public life, apart altogether from their necessary first-hand representation of the subjects intimately affecting the lives of women and children. The various philosophies and religions of India are at one in proclaiming "Woman may do what she can do." The veneration of the Orient for the Mother has reflected itself in the easy, respectful, happy, peaceful history to date of the Indian woman's desire for comradeship with man in every aspect of the struggle for freedom, individual, racial, and political. And India's supreme poet Rabindranath Tagore made his heroine Chitra say, "I am no goddess to be worshipped, nor yet the object of common pity to be brushed aside with indifference. Keep me by your side in the path of daring and danger, allow me to share the great duties of your life, then you will know my true self."

Mrs. Sakuntula Thampi

# Art in Early Indian Life

## By Mrs. Sakuntula Thampi

It is said that India reared a great spiritual civilization which made Alexander the great of Macedonia envious; indeed it must have been so, for if we examine her early architecture from the Buddhist Stupas, Fresco paintings, and sculptured "Gopurams" of the South and the peerless mausoleums of the North, we find that India's art went hand in hand with the religious instincts of her peoples.

The aesthetic and the religious blend in an admirable synthesis and this is India's noblest gift to humanity.

In painting, India has leapt forward. The Ajanta Frescoes of the 2nd century A. D. give us striking examples of the power and skill of those early artists. In their rock-cut retreat, a community of artist-monks, learned in religion as they were in art, produced their paintings, oblivious of communal strife or political unrest which ebbed and flowed in the country around. The oldest paintings therefore, represent no primitive beginning, but an art of some maturity. Here in the Ajanta caves, the onlooker will find a quality of art which is unique in itself, reaching degrees of sculpture together with painting unequalled in the recorded page. It stands for all that is creative, artistic and educative in the aesthetic instincts of our people in a great and glorious age, that has left its mark on the civilizations of the world.

And even more impressive than the noble paintings, are her carvings in stone, and her castings in bronze, of which India has been the greatest exponent in the world, for the inspiration of the Gupta-period, lasted long enough to influence the Dravidian architecture of the Seven Pagodas, and in the Mahratta country, we have the splendid caves of Ellora and Elephanta. In the gloom of these great caves are magnificent figures of Bramha, Vishnu, and Shiva; picture galleries in stone of epic tales and the cosmic activities of the Gods, depicting the art of stone-carving in its most graphic form. In the Southern temples of Madura, Chidambaram, and Tanjore are intricate columns, elaborate doorways, ceilings and pillars, with their exuberance of ornamentation, and complexity of design, which easily suggest the proud ambition, patience, and indefatigable energy which existed in early Dravidian sculpture and architecture.

Nowhere has religious philosophy so fused with art, as in the bronze figures of the God Nataraja, and it could be said with pride that no nation has ever produced a more intellectual symbolism embodied in the dance of creation.

Splendid dramas too educated the people, by such means, and by wandering minstrels were the Ramayana and the Maha Bharata, and the legends of Kalidasa and Shudraka expounded in the villages. Sometimes, under the patronage of kings, this great artistic-impulse continued. Dancing too in those early days was a subject

Antique Bronze figure of the God Nataraja Found in 1907 at Tiruvalangadu, Chittoor District. Now in the Madras Museum. Height 97 Centimetres.

of fervent literary appreciation, and believed to be religious, it was a part of the Temple rituals in the south, where religious, mystic, cosmic, and classic dances were practised and held in great significance and importance.

Music and song in those days were considered great accomplishments, and a great deal of time was spent in training the voice and the ear. We also find that together with sculpture, painting, drama, music and the dance, craftsmanship also flourished. A considerable amount of gold and silverware testify to the power and skill manifested by the early Indian jeweller. In Punjab and Rajputana, the silver chain bangles and anklets worn by the women are sometimes so beautifully finished that it would be impossible to believe that they were fashioned by human hands. Perhaps you have heard of the magic carpet owned by the Maharajah of Baroda? This is an entire carpet of pearls with gold corner pieces each weighing 514 tolas of gold, and closely studded with large diamonds; the united work of an excellent band of ancient Indian jewellers, and craftsmen. No aspect of early Indian art can have so much to teach as wood and ivory carving. Volumes on decorative art might in fact be written from a study of Indian carvings alone.

With early Indian textiles, embroideries, and handicrafts, we are on more familiar ground: their decorative effect and delicacy of execution single them out for universal admiration. These woven dreams are much sought after, and are as intrinsic in value as antiques in art and statuary.

I have seen some wonderful ancient specimens of Brocades, Kinkhawbs, Phulkaris, and Kashmiri Embroidery belonging to Mrs. Atiya Begum Fyazee at an Exhibition held at "Jingira Palace" Bombay, and Mrs. Kamala Devi Chattopadhyaya the well-known Indian politician is an ardent collector and connoisseur of Indian Embroideries and ancient hand-woven sarees which she often wears with great charm and dignity. Amongst the thinking few, Mrs. Kamala Devi found that it was but a poor exchange to trade our heritage for a memory, and was one of the first women pioneers to start an artistic revival in Indian textile-art. The delicate texture of ancient Dacca Muslins, the designs and colour-schemes of Ajanta and Sigirya, copies of Moghul and Persian Embroideries, South Indian prints and patterns of the past, were all sought out, and from a detailed study of these old masterpieces, an artistic regeneration of Indian textile art and handicrafts was founded.

There are marvellous venerable specimens of Oriental art and handicrafts in our several museums and palaces; to come in touch with them is to bridge the gulf of centuries, for though ages have passed, there still abides the memory of those ancients, whose genius wrought beauty and therefore joy, not only for their age, but for ours as well, who wrestled for days together, perhaps against tremendous odds to hand down unforgettable specimens of the artisan's craft; one cannot but behold with sympathy and admiration the rich legacy left to us.

Hand-Wrought Gold-bracelet of the early 15th century.
Set with Diamonds and Rubies.
Note "The Lotus Container" which unscrews revealing a tiny receptacle
made to contain Perfume and in more troublesome times poison was
carried by those who feared imprisonment or torture.

# Maharani Shree Jijabai Bhonsale

### (1595-1674. A. D.)

This famous lady was the mother of Shree Chhatrapati Shivaji Maharaj, the great founder of the Maratha Empire. Her life-sketch, it is hoped, will be an inspiration to Indian mothers in the present transitional period of our mother country.

This illustrious lady was born of the Jadhav House in the year 1595 A. D. The Jadhavas were the rulers of Deogiri and their rule was a "Golden Age" of Maharashtra. Statesmen, scientists and saints adorned their Court during the 13th century.

Evil days, however, fell on the House, and the Mohammedan power became supreme in the Deccan. The Jadhavas became subordinate commanders under the Muslim rulers of the Deccan. Lakhuji Jadhav— commander of considerable repute—was the father of Jijabai who thus inherited all the qualities of the Kshatriyas (Warrior race) in her veins.

She was married to Raje Shahaji Bhonsale in the year 1603 A. D. Jijabai was thus born and brought up in a Kshatriya House. The times were stirring, and she

His mother's inspiration. Shivaji.

witnessed them with open eyes and ears. She thought to herself that the only way of relief to her countrymen was through Swarajya and Swarajya alone.

She gave birth to several children of which two alone are known to History; Sambhaji and Shivaji. She paid particular attention to their training. They were brought up according to strict Hindu religious rites. The Life and Life-work of Shree Ramchandra—the hero of Ramayan—was constantly placed and preached before them by the mother. Early lessons were imparted in the military and administrative sciences known to the students of Indian History—"The Rise and Growth of the Maratha Power."

Jijabai thus gave a Shivaji to her country and all that it implies. She kept a watchful eye over all his deeds as he grew in years and prowess. It was through his mother's inspiration that Shivaji, the Great, turned his arms against the fort of Sinhagarh. She encouraged the poet Adnan Das to compose ballads on the exploits of Shivaji.

Social matters demanding adjustment did not escape her keen insight. Nimbalkar, a Kshatriya of strong arms and stout heart, had been forcibly converted to Islam. Jijabai summoned a Council of the prominent Marathas, placed and pleaded Nimbalkar's case before them and secured his entry back into the Hindu community. A great asset was thus gained to Shivaji's cause. She further led the way by marrying her granddaughter to the son of the said Nimbalkar.

Her son, Shivaji, the Great, grew both in fame and fortune. His affection and regard for his mother equalled his rise. He allotted a special department under her and in her service, her charities and patronage participated of parental solicitude for all her subjects.

A day dawned when all her motherly and national expectations were fulfilled under Divine Dispensation— the day of Shivaji's coronation, which was on the 13th day of the Bright Moon of Jeshtha according to the Hindu calendar. She was all busy and keen to arrange the ceremony on lines befitting her high ideal. Learned Pandits and brave and loyal warriors from all parts of India were invited and hospitably entertained to ensure the All-India nature of the great event.

Her life's mission was now fulfilled. Eleven days after the coronation of her son, she passed away at Pashan on the 29th day of the dark half of Jeshtha. Her ashes lie there.

The Vrindavan is a holy spot: this spot should be a place of pilgrimage to Indian mothers. The memory of this Royal mother styled as "the Life foundation of the country" and "Destroyer of the foe" by Ganga Bhatt, equally eminent in the cause of Swarajya and Swadharma shall ever be green.

With God's blessing may such great mothers adorn our Mother India.

# Women's Disabilities in Law

By Shyam Kumari Nehru

By H. H. Maharani Indirabai Holkar of Indore.

It is a notorious fact that Indian Women—whether Hindu or Muslim—suffer from various legal disabilities, and is assigned a definitely inferior position in law. The Women's movements in India are agitating for a better status for women and a more equitable state of things and social conditions are also full of promise for great changes ahead. But, wherever changes have taken place they are on an individual basis whereas for the mass of people the same old rigid laws and social rules hold good. Nevertheless, the laws as they exist inflict a world of hardship in various cases that come to light almost every day in a lawyer's chambers and in the law courts.

The position assigned to women in the laws of the country is very one-sided. The provisions of the Indian Penal Code with reference to abduction, kidnapping and adultery become ludicrous in some cases and yet in an inelastic system of administration where past cases decide the fate of future problems there is almost no place for a changing world. In an interesting case, a woman was the cause of the conviction of three men and the circumstances speak volumes for themselves. The Woman aged 35 and mother of four children was alleged to have been enticed away from the lawful custody of her husband! The truth of the matter was that she could not pull on with her husband, but she could not escape from his clutches as the law did not permit separation between the couple and there was no custom to over-ride the law; so she desperately appealed to her friends in the village and their only crime was that they helped her out of a hopeless situation. They were moved by humane considerations and it was nobody's case that there were any other motives behind their help, and yet, the law had to be fulfilled and they stood convicted of a criminal offence! The Judge in the appellate court was a man with imagination and he released the accused after awarding a technical punishment, but it is a strange commentary on the Penal Code that there was no option left to the Judge but to convict!

Another set of laws that inflict a very great deal of hardship in modern society are those relating to Marriage, Divorce and Bigamy. Society is advancing and modern age is full of mixed marriages and yet there is no change in the Civil Marriage Act which was enacted in the 19th century for the benefit of the Brahma Samaj that believed in neither Hinduism, Islam, Buddhism or Zoroastrianism. Dr. Gour's amendment has made an exception in certain conditions but its range is very limited. The result is that where parties belong to different religions other than Hinduism, Jainism, Buddhism or Sikhism they must declare that they do not profess their respective religions. In one case the parties were religious minded and believed in their respective religions with the result that they contracted a marriage completely invalid in law, in the hope that such examples as theirs would help in the creation of a purely civil marriage act that would not take into consideration the religions of the respective parties.

Another cause for a great deal of hardship is the absence of Divorce in Hindu Law except where it is customary among the lower classes. Hindu and Muslim marriages are polygamous and are consequently not recognised as valid marriages in English law, which recognises only monogamous unions. The result is a regular crop of cases in which Hindu and Muslim young men of middle-class families have coolly abandoned their first wives and contracted civil marriages with European women abroad. The discarded wives have no redress in law except that they can claim maintenance allowance and, more often than not, the maintenance given is so paltry that a self-respecting woman refuses to take it! About half a dozen cases have come to light recently of such second marriages, and in one case the hardship on the woman was all the severe as she had been married as a child and never seen her husband afterwards. The husband was sent for a higher education abroad and came back with a German wife. This young girl was thus relegated to the miserable life of a child widow and her parents were helpless as there was no redress in law.

There was another very pitiable case in which the father of a young girl of 18 went almost mad with grief. He married his daughter at the age of 12 into a family that was desirable from every social standard—and the young man was a student full of promise for the future.

But things did not turn out to be as bright as they seemed; the father of the girl was poor, he could not satisfy the demands of the boy's family, and very soon after the marriage the girl was sent back to her father's home. The boy was brilliant, and was the cynosure of all eyes— quietly he was remarried into a richer family—and the first wife was told that she was not needed any longer. The father of the girl went almost mad with rage, he felt like a criminal for having ruined the life of his daughter and he desperately approached lawyers to find a way out. His demand was that he should be able to re-marry his daughter to a very eligible young man who was sporting enough to ask for her hand in marriage—but—he wanted the young man to escape from the clutches of the Penal Code and offered to go to jail himself for committing the offence of re-marrying his daughter in the life-time of her husband. No lawyer could satisfy the demands of the grief-stricken father, the law ran its full course—and the girl was condemned to a life of perpetual widowhood for no fault of her own.

In another case the father of the girl was very rich and he had an only daughter. She was unfortunately wedded to an invalid who was also a libertine. The only interest of the husband in the wife was to get as much as he possibly could—out of her. The father and daughter were both disgusted and wanted to find some way out of the marriage tie. Being Hindus, the marriage was indissoluble. Lawyers were consulted and a change of religion was even tried. But the son-in-law could not possibly give up the golden calf and he followed in the footsteps of his wife by a similar change of religion. There was thus no way out for her and she was compelled to resign herself to fate.

There is another social tragedy being enacted in a particular home. Husband and wife have lived happily together for 12 years but unfortunately the marriage has not resulted in any issue. The husband is now thinking of re-marriage for the sake of a child and the wife is completely helpless faced with the prospect of being turned out on the streets with a pittance, or with being relegated to the kitchen of some rich relation's household, serving the family well in order to earn the right of residence and food.

All these cases reveal a very one-sided system of laws and—it can be safely asserted that in both the Hindu and Muslim legal systems a great deal of hardship is inflicted on the women. Even in the Muslim Shariat Law the woman is given an inferior position though it must be admitted that she enjoys a comparative measure of greater freedom and more rights. Nevertheless, in almost all walks of life, it is the woman who pays most. The social movements in India are now clamouring for women's rights and slowly but surely a revolution is taking place in Indian social conditions. There is therefore hope for the future if women will realise their position and unite to improve it. The Indian Woman of today is being put to the severest test. She has to reconcile various conflicting ideals—born in a rigid state of things she is given sufficient education to appreciate freedom and progress and yet she is bound by fetters of convention and law. Slowly she is shaking off her chains and there is little doubt that she will emerge glorious and free.

# Indian Indigenous Industries

By Jayashriben Raiji

The problem of industrialization of India has been in the forefront of public discussion. The ministers of Industries in all the provinces have been exercising their minds seriously over this question. Industrial awakening is going on apace in India and it still needs better organisation and more encouragement from the public. It cannot be emphasised too often that in India, the foundation of National progress must be happiness, welfare and prosperity of the dwellers in seven lakhs of our villages. With her huge agricultural population idle for more than half of every year, India presents the greatest unemployment problem of the world. It is now over fifty years since the Famine Commission of 1880 urged "the development of Industries other than agriculture and independent of the fluctuations of the season." If India is to prosper, it is essential that the rural population should have a diversity of occupations. Hence it is that cottage industries have occupied an important place in the national economy of all countries, especially those that are predominantly agricultural. Everywhere it is recognised that the handicrafts have a cultural value of their own in preserving and developing the skill and inherent artistic capabilities of the humblest individual. In India their role in national economy is all the more important, for as we have seen our problem is to carry the industries to our farms and to combine industry with agriculture.

Until the advent of machinery, all production was carried on through cottage industries which were either full-time or part-time occupations. This was the old-world economy all over the world, but especially in India where in the words of a British writer "a busy population had covered the land with the marks of industry... Skilled artisans converted the rude products of the soil into fabrics of unrivalled delicacy and beauty." The Cambridge History of Ancient India observes "Silks, muslins, the finer sorts of cloth, cutlery and armour, brocade, embroideries and ivory work, jewellery and gold, these were the Indian articles in which the merchants dealt." If we examine these lists carefully, we find, however, one marked difference in the general character between the trade of India today, and that of about three thousand years ago. India was principally an exporter of manufactures. The most prominent example is of course that of cotton. India's age-old mastery of cotton manufacture has been vividly expressed by a European writer of the sixteenth century who remarks: "Every one from Cape of Good Hope to China is clothed from head to foot by the products of the Indian looms." Apart from textiles the most important category of manufactures exported from India was metal-ware, principally iron and steel goods. India must have reached a very high stage of manufacturing skill in iron at a very early date. Even during the Moghul period the volume as well as the value of the Indian trade was considerable. The great bulk of the commerce in the Indian seas was carried in ships built in India. Ship-building was a most important industry in the Mohammedan and the Hindu periods. Thus the "Wealth that was Ind" in the days of the Hindu and Mussalman Emperors was the creation of a flourishing industry in all departments of human wants, a profitable foreign trade based on this industry and a wise far-sighted system of Government.

By the imposition of heavy duties on the import into England of Indian manufactures, the granting of special privileges to British companies importing their own goods into India, the forcing on India of a fiscal policy opposed to its interests, all these industries were ruthlessly crushed a century ago. The one-sided free-trade policy resulted in the ruin and total extinction of many of India's staple industries and drove millions of her children out of employment. The heaviest injury of this free-trade policy fell, however, not on Indian capitalists, but on her handicraft workers. Very gradually, yet by an irresistible doom, the weaver, the potter and the smith were reduced to penury and despair, by the competition of British machines. So far as India was concerned the good opportunity for fostering her industries undisturbed by foreign competition presented itself to her during the world war and several of the industries made a rapid progress. This was followed by the fiscal autonomy convention granted to her in 1919, under which she could, to a limited extent, impose customs duties on foreign imports. The swadeshi movement that followed gave a still greater impetus to these industries, and imports began rapidly to decline. It is in order to counteract this difficulty that foreign owned and foreign controlled, particularly English, factories are dumped in India. A huge cry has gone up against the growing invasion of India by foreign capital and the rapid establishment in this country of more and more industrial concerns under the control and management of foreigners and the consequent capturing by them of the fields in which Indian industries till now have been struggling to grow. That is the reason why the Congress has demanded the right and power to discriminate in favour of national against non-nationals when Indian interests require it.

Shrijut Subhas Bose, President of the Indian National Congress has recently said that the main problems with which they had to contend were slavery, poverty and unemployment. We wanted to end exploitation and the first duty of the Swaraj government would be the provision of bread to millions. Shrijut Bose referred to the National Planning Scheme. He assured the public that industrialisation and rural development, in which Gandhiji was keenly interested, would continue side by side and cottage industries would be properly looked after. With the acceptance of Khaddar as the national uniform the Congress has evinced in a practical manner its identification with the cause of the economic uplift of the rural population and the national demand for the boycott of foreign cloth has acquired a new significance. Similarly the national urge for swadeshi underwent a transformation when the congress resolved at its session in Bombay to confine the energies of its workers to the promotion of a campaign for the increase of production in villages and for an extension of the use of village-made products. It is one of the principal objects of the All-India Village Industries Association to provide technical advice and guidance and, as its resources grow, it expects to make these services increasingly available for the development of various cottage industries in different parts of the country. A training class of workers has already been opened at Wardha and investigations have been taken in hand into the conditions and requirements of various industries such as oil-pressing, paper manufacturing and tanning, etc.

Good as these attempts may be in keeping alive some art-crafts, the total contribution of these exports to the national income must be insignificant. What is more necessary is to check the import and use of foreign manufactures, such as clothing, sugar, salt, steel that our people used to manufacture for themselves. There are in the first place certain industries like cement and steel, which can only be conducted successfully on a large scale by employing modern methods and machinery which are beyond the scope of cottage industries. It is certainly true that the employment of modern agencies like electric energy or quicker methods like those adopted in spinning mills would largely implement many of our cottage industries and produce better results. But that is neither a plea for abolition of cottage industries nor a justification of universal adoption of large scale and mechanised industrialisation. There is yet another group of industries where if modern and up-to-date methods of manufacture were not introduced, they could hardly have survived the competition of cheaper machine made goods from abroad. There are yet some other industries where the adoption of large scale manufacture may be forced upon us by the contingency that unless we do it we may be forestalled by foreign enterprise in India. Some cottage industries may suffer, but there will remain many others which are not in any peril of destruction through the competition of cheaper imported goods. A few may require some kind of protection against even Indian machine-made goods. We may have also to give special encouragement to village industries against competition of urban factories for the manufacture of goods in constant local demand for which the villages possess obvious advantages. Besides, it may be found possible to give an impetus to small and cottage industries by opening up subsidiary lines in connection with the large organised industries. The villages may in this way be connected with industrial centres and play a significant and more effective role in the industrial expansion of the country.

Let us examine the situation in the country of some of the most important industries. Jute, Sugar, Cement, Coal, etc., have reached the stage of over-production relatively to the existing level of demand while certain other industries such as cotton, textile, iron and steel, paper, soap and glass have yet possibilities of further expansion under certain favourable conditions. There are quite a number of other industries for which India possesses very good potentialities, but which could not be exploited for want of adequate fiscal protection or other forms of Government assistance; while there are some others like the generation of hydro-electric power, manufacture of petrol from coal, etc., the potentialities of which remain yet to be fully investigated.

Under popular ministers in the provinces systematic efforts are being made to introduce compulsory free primary education and other developmental services such as rural uplift, adult education etc., which are bound to create increased demand in the country for many articles, such as, broad-casting apparatus and various writing materials. Such nation-building activities of the Provincial Governments will throw open new lines of profitable industry.

In the present stage of industrial development in India it would be a sufficient fillip to rapid expansion if adequate assistance is provided in the following directions. The first necessity is for making a comprehensive survey to find out the most suitable channels along which our enterprise for industrial expansion should be directed. In this due attention will have to be paid to the availability of raw materials, extent of the market and other necessary requisites. Secondly, such industries which have the best scope for growth should be given adequate protection to prevent their being stifled by foreign competition. Thirdly, it may be necessary to foster the growth of basic industries by direct financial assistance. Fourthly, for the smaller and cottage industries the State should maintain an adequate machinery for rendering expert advice on improved technique of production, providing cheaper credit and better marketing facilities and furthering the co-operative movements.

While calling upon the State to do its duty, the public should not forget that they too owe a duty to the primary producers in our towns and villages. The public can help this in various ways. They can form district associations to study the problems of local industries, conduct surveys, frame programmes of development, organise museums and exhibitions, assist in organising the producers, preferably on a co-operative basis, link-up these associations with research workshops, arrange for the supply of raw materials and appliances and place them in touch with the markets in urban centres. They should go a step further and actively canvass support for the products of these industries and patronize the producers themselves. All effort at national regeneration necessarily involves some sacrifice. Our Indian women are well-known for their spirit of sacrifice, and no sacrifice is too great for the freedom of our motherland.